Name _____

INNOVATIONS

The Comprehensive Preschool Curriculum:

Teacher's Guide

The Comprehensive
Preschool
CURRICULUM

Teacher's
Guide

Linda G. Miller / Kay Albrecht ●

Dedication

This book is dedicated to all of the talented early childhood educators and trainers who showed us the way to bring adult education to life for teachers in training.

Copyright

All rights reserved

Photographs: Masami Mizukami

Bulk purchase

Gryphon House books are available at special discount when purchased in bulk for special premiums and sales promotions as well as for fund-raising use. Special editions or book excerpts also can be created to specification. For details, contact the Director of Marketing.

Disclaimer

The publisher and the authors cannot be held responsible for injury, mishap, or damages incurred during the use of or because of the activities in this book. The authors recommend appropriate and reasonable supervision at all times based on the age and development of each child.

Table of Contents

Introduction

Today you are beginning a new adventure to support what you do in the classroom with preschool children. ***Innovations: The Comprehensive Preschool Curriculum: Teacher's Guide*** is designed to provide over 40 hours of professional development for teachers using ***Innovations: The Comprehensive Preschool Curriculum***. While completing the modules in this book, you will have opportunities to explore all the different elements of curriculum that impact young children and how they grow and learn.

In addition to exploring the book and learning about all its different features, you will also get a chance to use the curriculum forms, activities, and webs, and explore teaching knowledge to support young children's development and educational achievement. By the time you complete the Teacher's Guide, you will have a thorough understanding of all of the components of curriculum.

The modules in this book are designed to be completed by an individual teacher with the support (hopefully) of a mentor, trainer, director, or principal. Each module contains a partial checklist of skills to assure that skills you learn in training are being implemented in the classroom and integrated into your teaching skills repertoire. Modules are designed to be completed in the sequence they appear. Unless noted otherwise, all page numbers in this book are references to *Innovations: The Comprehensive Preschool Curriculum*.

We hope you enjoy your adventure both in completing this training and in enriching the lives of young children and their families. Write your name on the title page of this book, and let's get started!

Best wishes,

Linda G. Miller   Kay Albrecht

Welcome and Purpose of Training

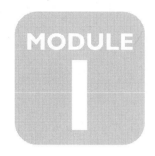

MODULE 1

Purpose: to introduce *Innovations: The Comprehensive Preschool Curriculum: Teacher's Guide* including assumptions, reasons for teaching, and philosophy of education

TIME: APPROXIMATELY 1 HOUR

Introduction

Innovations: The Comprehensive Preschool Curriculum: Teacher's Guide is designed to help teachers prepare to use *Innovations: The Comprehensive Preschool Curriculum* in the classroom.

Beginning teachers will learn step by step about early care and education for preschool children. They will learn how young children learn, how to create an appropriate learning environment, how to include parents in the lives of their children at school, and how to ensure basic health and classroom safety. Beginning teachers will learn the basics of providing care and early education for preschool children. Experienced teachers will have opportunities to learn new curriculum ideas and to understand evidenced-based best practices in care and early education. All teachers will be challenged to perfect their skills in interaction, curriculum development, observation, and documentation.

Assumptions

This teacher-training guide is based on the following assumptions:

- *All teachers need initial, as well as on-going training—no matter what level of formal education they have achieved*. Life-long learning is important for everyone, especially teachers. New research in the area of care and early education provides updated insight into how young children grow and learn.

- *Parents are their children's first and most important teachers*. Parents have a stronger and more lasting effect on their children than anyone or anything else. Relationships with important adults determine how safe a child feels, how a child feels about himself or herself, how a child relates to others, and his or her readiness to learn.

- *In addition to their parents, children's teachers are of primary importance in their young lives*. A preschool child's teacher is a significant adult in terms of providing quality interactions and facilitating emotional and social development. Additionally, teachers have a direct influence on a child's language, cognitive, and physical development.

- *Children's initial experiences with adults are critical in determining how they will relate to others, how they will feel about themselves, and how they will perform academically*. Teachers support children's learning in all domains

of development as they understand individual differences, scaffold learning, and support the exploration of ideas and interests.

- **All children deserve to be in an environment where they are safe, loved, and learning**. The early years are learning years. Success during the preschool years predicts future academic success. Children are constructing their own knowledge from their interactions and experiences at home, at school, and in the community at large.

- **Being involved in the lives of young children and their families through teaching is an enriching and stimulating experience**. Because "We are shaped and fashioned by what we love" (Goethe), being involved in the lives of young children and their families can be very special and fulfilling.

Why teach? Use the space below to explain why you teach (or want to teach) preschool children.

What are your beliefs about how you should educate young children?

Teacher Completing Training Module   Date
(Please sign and date)

Congratulations! You have completed Module 1 in the **Teacher's Guide**.

Get Acquainted with *Innovations: The Comprehensive Preschool Curriculum*

Purpose: to become familiar with *Innovations: The Comprehensive Preschool Curriculum*

TIME: APPROXIMATELY 1 HOUR

During this module, you will have an opportunity to get to know how *Innovations: The Comprehensive Preschool Curriculum* is organized. (You might find it helpful to use different colors of stick-on notes or flags to create tabs, so you can turn quickly to the different sections of the book.)

Chapter 1—Getting Started (pages 15-30) provides an overview of the entire book. Read the chapter. Then find and read the following sections, which show a variety of what the book offers. Use the Table of Contents, Appendix (pages 557-618), and the Index (pages 619-634) to find the page numbers. Write the page numbers below.

Page Number	Book Section
_____	Chapter 3—Making Friends
_____	Possibilities Plan: *Building Up and Tearing Down*
_____	Possibilities Plan: *Saying Hello*
_____	Chapter 4—Exploring Roles
_____	Observation Classroom Summary
_____	Concepts Learned Classroom Summary
_____	Child Accomplishment Record

You will have many more opportunities to get to know the book as you continue with your training in the Teacher's Guide.

_____   _____

Teacher Completing Training Module   Date
(Please sign and date)

Congratulations! You have completed Module 2 in the *Teacher's Guide*.

Personal Goals for Professional Development

Purpose: to create your professional development goals, including goals related to curriculum planning, observation and assessment, and early childhood education

TIME: APPROXIMATELY 1 HOUR

Innovations: The Comprehensive Preschool Curriculum is unique in that it views curriculum in a very broad sense. As you complete this guide, you will learn about all of the following aspects of curriculum that influence preschool children.

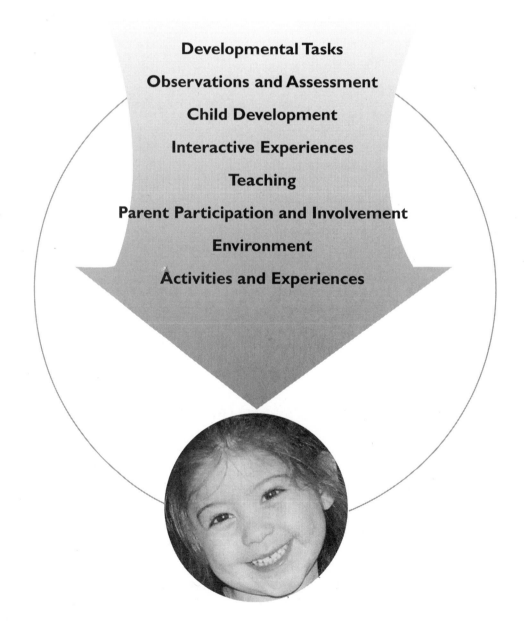

Developmental Tasks

Observations and Assessment

Child Development

Interactive Experiences

Teaching

Parent Participation and Involvement

Environment

Activities and Experiences

As a teacher it is important for you to set goals. This module will give you an opportunity to do so in specific areas related to your *Innovations* training. You may find it helpful to review Chapter 1—Getting Started (pages 15-30) as you write your goals.

My goal for activities and experiences is to:
(for example, learn five new activities in each Possibilities area, add science activities to my curriculum planning, or try one project with children)

My curriculum planning goal is to:
(for example, add webbing to the planning process I use, invite parents to participate in webbing as part of my curriculum planning, or collect the materials for five prop boxes)

My observation and assessment goal is to:
(for example, complete one observation on each child each week, or use observations to assess children's development)

My early childhood education goal is to:
(for example, understand the behaviors associated with different developmental ages and stages, or help parents understand children's ages and stages and the impact of age and stage on parenting)

What role will your mentor or trainer* (see the next page) play in your professional development?
(for example, my mentor will observe me twice a week and complete the checklists in the *Teacher's Guide*, talk with me about each module, and so on.)

3

* All teachers need someone to talk with and discuss issues concerning the classroom. Individuals can complete this teacher's guide independently, but interaction with a mentor or trainer will make this a more powerful professional experience. In the space below, identify the person you will use as a resource. Consider asking a more experienced teacher, a supervisor, an education professor, a community college teacher, a director, or a consultant from a resource and referral agency.

My mentor or trainer is _____.
Her/his telephone number is_____.
Her/his email address is_____.
Her/his mailing address is _____.

Skills Checklist

If you are currently working in the classroom, ask your mentor to support your development by observing your growing skills. For now, ask your mentor to observe only for the skills listed below. Then, as you complete additional modules and learn new skills and abilities, use the complete list on pages 105-107 of this book to confirm that you are developing your teaching skills repertoire. If you are unfamiliar with an item, read about it in the book or talk further with your mentor or trainer. If you are not currently teaching, become familiar with the concepts and save the lists to use when you are teaching in a preschool program.

_____ Participates in professional development experiences
_____ Keeps record of professional development experiences
_____ Sets short-term and long-term goals for professional development
_____ Practices safety precautions in the classroom (for example, attendance taken, children never left alone, allergy list posted, toys and materials regularly checked for safety) (see pages 384-386, 504)
Note: This skill appears here out of sequence because these are important safety considerations for any teacher in the classroom.

_____   _____

Teacher Completing Training Module   Date
(Please sign and date)

_____   _____

Trainer or Mentor Completing Skills Checklist   Date
(Please sign and date)

Congratulations! You have completed Module 3 in the **Teacher's Guide**.

Developmental Tasks

Purpose: to learn about the developmental tasks included in *Innovations: The Comprehensive Preschool Curriculum*

TIME: APPROXIMATELY 1 HOUR

Development is a lifelong task. It begins in infancy and continues throughout one's lifespan. There are many different ideas about how humans develop into capable, productive, functional adults. *Innovations: The Comprehensive Preschool Curriculum* proposes six life tasks that begin in infancy and continue as development emerges. Each life task is grounded in theory and the resulting practices that have emerged from developmental and interactional theory and research, and from our current understanding of how children learn. Developmental tasks show how children develop in similar ways and also how each child's development is unique.

Developmental tasks in *Innovations: The Comprehensive Preschool Curriculum* are loosely sequential from Chapter 2 through Chapter 7. Because developmental tasks are broad in nature, they often encompass several, or even all of the components of child development (physical, intellectual, emotional, and social).

Developmental Tasks by Age

Birth–18 Months	18 Months–36 Months	3–5 Years
Separating from Parents ⟶	Transitioning to School ⟶	Adjusting to School
Connecting to School ⟶	Making Friends ⟶	
Relating to Self and Others ⟶	Exploring Roles ⟶	
⟵ Communicating with Parents, Teachers, and Friends ⟶		
Moving Around ⟶	Problem-solving ⟶	
⟵ Expressing Feelings with Parents, Teachers, and Friends ⟶		

Read about developmental tasks in Chapter 1, page 16. Then, take some time to read about the different developmental tasks in *Innovations: The Comprehensive Preschool Curriculum*. Notice that each chapter in the book relates to a developmental task. (For example, Adjusting to School is Chapter 2.) Write the chapter number by the developmental tasks listed below and identify why each developmental task is important for preschool children.

Adjusting to School: Chapter _____

Making Friends: Chapter _____

Exploring Roles: Chapter _____

Communicating with Parents, Teachers, and Friends: Chapter _____

Problem Solving: Chapter _____

Expressing Feelings with Parents, Teachers, and Friends: Chapter _____

Skills Checklist

If you are currently working in the classroom, ask your mentor to support your development by observing your growing skills. For now, ask your mentor to observe only for the skills listed below. Then, as you complete additional modules and learn new skills and abilities, use the complete list on pages 105-107 of this book to confirm that you are developing your teaching skills repertoire. If you are unfamiliar with an item, read about it in the book or talk further with your mentor or trainer. If you are not currently teaching, become familiar with the concepts and save the lists to use when you are teaching in a preschool program.

_____ Delights in each child's success and expresses kindness and support when children are struggling with developmental challenges (see pages 495-496)

_____ Recognizes and supports developmental tasks in the classroom (pages 37-38)

_____ Practices safety precautions in the classroom

_____   _____
Teacher Completing Training Module   Date
(Please sign and date)

_____   _____
Trainer or Mentor Completing Skills Checklist   Date
(Please sign and date)

Congratulations! You have completed Module 4 in the **Teacher's Guide**.

MODULE 5

Innovations in Care and Early Education

Purpose: to understand how child development and early childhood education principles, theories, and practices inform teaching

TIME: APPROXIMATELY 1½ HOURS

Each chapter includes a section on the underlying theory or child development principles, best practices, and/or content knowledge explaining developmental tasks. Read about Innovations in Care and Early Education on page 17 in Chapter 1—Getting Started. In each chapter, these sections build knowledge and skills to support children's growth and development. Some topics include transitioning to school, primary teaching, literacy development, temperament, and social development theories. Innovations in Care and Early Education helps explain why children behave in different ways.

Sometimes teachers view children's behaviors in isolation. However, underlying early childhood principles give us rationales and theoretical explanations of why children behave in particular ways. The following chart shows the relationship between three common "challenges" in the classroom and the care and early education topics related to them.

Classroom Challenges	Care and Early Education Topics
Hitting	Social problem solving (pages 135-137)
Aggression	Emotional behavior (pages 479-495)
Discipline problems	Internalization of self-control (pages 477-478)

Choose a classroom challenge with which you need help or one in which you are interested. Write the topic here.

Use the table of contents or index to find section(s) that relate to your topic. Read them and write the page numbers for the sections here.

How can knowing about care and early education help with the classroom challenge you chose?

Identify a resource you can use to read further. Write it here.

> [blank box]

In researching the challenge you identified, you may have discovered a best practice—a commonly held approach for early childhood professionals to use in their classrooms (for example, telling children why you are going to do something, providing outdoor play time each day, and so on). Write the best practice here.

> [blank box]

Skills Checklist

If you are currently working in the classroom, ask your mentor to support your development by observing your growing skills. For now, ask your mentor to observe only for the skills listed below. Then, as you complete additional modules and learn new skills and abilities, use the complete list on pages 105-107 of this book to confirm that you are developing your teaching skills repertoire. If you are unfamiliar with an item, read about it in the book or talk further with your mentor or trainer. If you are not currently teaching, become familiar with the concepts and save the lists to use when you are teaching in a preschool program.

_____ Allows children some flexibility in following routines; does not insist on scheduling compliance that conflicts with individual schedules (see pages 133, 141)

_____ Does not treat every child the same—bases interactions and teaching on understanding of each child's developmental age and stage as well as on the child's uniqueness (see pages 40-42)

_____ Uses non-punitive ways of dealing with behavior; can exert authority without requiring submission or undermining the child's sense of self (see pages 129-130)

_____   _____
Teacher Completing Training Module   Date
(Please sign and date)

_____   _____
Trainer or Mentor Completing Skills Checklist   Date
(Please sign and date)

Congratulations! You have completed Module 5 in the **Teacher's Guide**.

Innovations in Interactive Experiences

Purpose: to practice using the interactive experiences provided in each chapter of *Innovations: The Comprehensive Preschool Curriculum*

TIME: APPROXIMATELY 1 HOUR

Children's experiences in school have so much to do with the way they grow and develop. If they experience school as negative, frustrating, or insensitive, they view the learning process as overwhelming. If, on the other hand, their relationships and experiences at school are supportive, nurturing, and positive, human development has an almost perfect plan for growing and learning.

This curriculum advocates thinking about and planning for everything that can, by the nature of the setting (school vs. home), contribute to children's learning and development, and the teacher's relationship with the child and family. Further, it grounds planning in a developmental, interactional, theoretical framework. Finally, it views all children's experiences, not just formal educational experiences, as important learning opportunities.

Interactive experiences may be serendipitous and often spontaneous. They are an important part of the curriculum plan and include types of experiences that you, as the teacher, keep in mind to support and provide across the school day. Read about interactive experiences on pages 17-18 in Chapter 1—Getting Started. Also, each chapter (2-7) offers a section called Innovations in Interactive Experiences. These sections discuss the relationship between interactive experiences and the developmental tasks. Read about the interactive experiences related to the developmental task of Adjusting to School, pages 44-47. Then read the list below.

1. Prepare children for transitions. Talk with children about what is going to happen to them next. Use songs, fingerplays, and rhymes to support transitions.
2. In full-day programs, leave written records for other teachers who are involved in children's care and early education. Written records prevent relying solely on verbal exchanges that may get lost in the midst of transitions.
3. Watch your tone of voice and your non-verbal cues during interactions. Congruence between what you say and the way you say it, and what you do and the way you do it, is communication.

4. Support children during new experiences. When new things are happening in the school environment, children need support in taking in the new stimuli. Sometimes this support is anticipatory, such as warning children that the fire alarm is going to go off in a minute, or reminding children that you are going to ask them to stop what they are doing and go outside.

5. Know each child's temperament and learning style, so you can anticipate what each child will need. When physical support is no longer needed, visually support the child with eye contact and non-verbal cues such as smiling and nodding your head.

Which of these interactive experiences are you already incorporating in your classroom on a regular basis?

Which experiences do you need to incorporate into your interactions?

How will you do this?

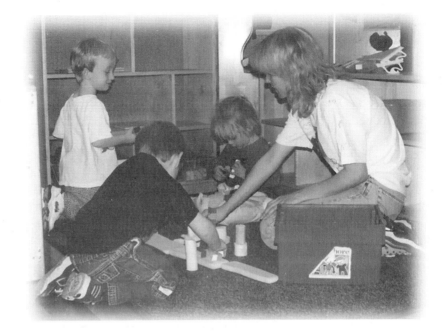

Skills Checklist

If you are currently working in the classroom, ask your mentor to support your development by observing your growing skills. For now, ask your mentor to observe only for the skills listed below. Then, as you complete additional modules and learn new skills and abilities, use the complete list on pages 105-107 of this book to confirm that you are developing your teaching skills repertoire. If you are unfamiliar with an item, read about it in the book or talk further with your mentor or trainer. If you are not currently teaching, become familiar with the concepts and save the lists to use when you are teaching in a preschool program.

_____Actively seeks meaningful exchanges with children (see page 301)
_____Waits for responses to questions (see page 301)
_____Asks open-ended questions that require more than a one-word response
        (see pages 308-309)

Teacher Completing Training Module   Date
(Please sign and date)

Trainer or Mentor Completing Skills Checklist   Date
(Please sign and date)

Congratulations! You have completed Module 6 in the **Teacher's Guide**.

Innovations in Teaching

MODULE 7

Purpose: to support the development of different teacher roles and teacher competencies by using the Innovations in Teaching sections in the chapters

TIME: APPROXIMATELY 1 HOUR

First, read about Innovations in Teaching in Chapter 1—Getting Started, page 18. Additionally, each subsequent chapter (2-7) contains a section called Innovations in Teaching (pages 48-51, 132-139, 216-221, 303-311, 398-406, 488-496), which discusses practices that are important in the classroom and the teacher's important role in the classroom. Also included in the section is a checklist of Teacher Competencies to use as a self-evaluation, peer evaluation, or evaluation by a mentor or trainer. Most items here are taken from the Teacher Competencies Checklist in each chapter of **Innovations: The Comprehensive Preschool Curriculum**. A section called Resources for Teachers is located within each chapter to encourage additional reading and research.

From the Resources for Teachers listed in Chapter 4 (page 234), choose a resource that will help you learn more about a topic of interest. Write it down here.

In Chapter 2, read Innovations in Teaching (pages 48-51) and Temperament (pages 38-40). Then complete the following activity: Observe one child in your classroom. Mark each item on the Temperament Chart on the next page. Temperamental characteristics are described on a continuum from low to high. Use the results to determine if the child is predominantly flexible, fearful, or feisty. Discuss your findings with your mentor or trainer.

Temperament Chart

Mark where each child's behaviors fall on the continuum. Use this information to help you plan.

1) activity level

2) regularity of biological rhythms (sleeping, eating, and elimination)

3) approach/withdrawal tendencies

4) mood, positive to negative

5) intensity of reaction

6) adaptability

7) sensitivity to light, touch, taste, sound, and sights

8) distractibility

9) persistence

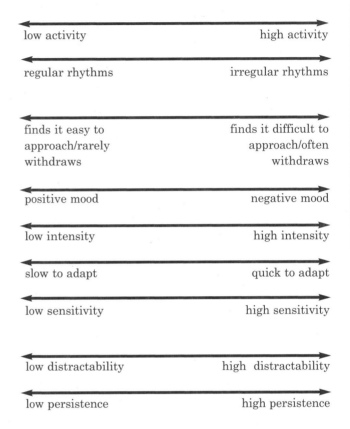

low activity ←——————————————→ high activity

regular rhythms ←——————————————→ irregular rhythms

finds it easy to approach/rarely withdraws ←——————————————→ finds it difficult to approach/often withdraws

positive mood ←——————————————→ negative mood

low intensity ←——————————————→ high intensity

slow to adapt ←——————————————→ quick to adapt

low sensitivity ←——————————————→ high sensitivity

low distractability ←——————————————→ high distractability

low persistence ←——————————————→ high persistence

Adapted from California State Department of Education (1990). *Flexible, fearful, or feisty: The different temperaments of infants and toddlers.* Videotape. Sacramento, CA: Department of Education.

Use the Temperament Chart to gain insight into the behaviors of children in the classroom and modify your teaching roles to support individual development.

What did you determine about the child's temperament?

Skills Checklist

If you are currently working in the classroom, ask your mentor to support your development by observing your growing skills. For now, ask your mentor to observe only for the skills listed below. Then, as you complete additional modules and learn new skills and abilities, use the complete list on pages 105-107 of this book to confirm that you are developing your teaching skills repertoire. If you are unfamiliar with an item, read about it in the book or talk further with your mentor or trainer. If you are not currently teaching, become familiar with the concepts and save the lists to use when you are teaching in a preschool program.

_____ Shows with nonverbal and verbal cues that she or he likes children and teaching (see pages 470-473)

_____ Knows and uses a variety of guidance techniques such as redirection, distraction, ignoring; uses room arrangement and schedules to support appropriate behavior; uses each approach appropriately (see pages 129-130)

_____ Plans, implements, and evaluates parent-teacher conferences (pages 56-58), intake interviews, and gradual enrollment (see pages 48-49)

_____   _____

Teacher Completing Training Module   Date
(Please sign and date)

_____   _____

Trainer or Mentor Completing Skills Checklist   Date
(Please sign and date)

Congratulations! You have completed Module 7 in the **Teacher's Guide**.

MODULE 8

Innovations in Observation and Assessment

Purpose: to view observation and assessment as the foundation of understanding children's development and experiences

TIME: APPROXIMATELY 1 HOUR

Three components of observation and assessment are necessary to inform curriculum planning:

- Careful observation of children at work and at play
- Information gathered from developmental checklists or assessment instruments
- Documentation of children's growth and learning

Each chapter in *Innovations: The Comprehensive Preschool Curriculum* contains a section called Innovations in Observation and Assessment. This section shows how observation and assessment are related to the chapter's developmental task. Additionally, teachers are given ideas for work samples to add to children's portfolios, providing both documentation of children's skill acquisition and another opportunity to conduct individual assessment by analyzing children's knowledge construction.

Children's learning is not linear. Development is sporadic in nature and proceeds in fits and starts. Systematic observation gives teachers insight into how each child's development is unfolding, as well as an understanding of developmental uniqueness.

First, read about Innovations in Observation and Assessment in Chapter 1—Getting Started (pages 18-19). Next, read Innovations in Observation and Assessment in Chapter 5—Communicating with Parents, Teachers, and Friends (pages 312-315). What did you learn? Write three ideas here.

1. _____

2. _____

3. _____

To continue this module, choose an activity or experience to observe in the classroom. Later in this *Teacher's Guide* you will get more experience with both observation and curriculum development.

Which activity or experience did you choose? (include page number)

What did you observe?

Use your observation to determine which developmental tasks the child is working on.

Developmental Task _____
Why?

Developmental Task _____
Why?

Developmental Task _____
Why?

Skills Checklist

If you are currently working in the classroom, ask your mentor to support your development by observing your growing skills. For now, ask your mentor to observe only for the skills listed below. Then, as you complete additional modules and learn new skills and abilities, use the complete list on pages 105-107 of this book to confirm that you are developing your teaching skills repertoire. If you are unfamiliar with an item, read about it in the book or talk further with your mentor or trainer. If you are not currently teaching, become familiar with the concepts and save the lists to use when you are teaching in a preschool program.

_____ Structures time for observation into daily or weekly teaching routines (see pages 46-47)

_____ Uses observation to inform curriculum planning and provide insight into interactions with children (see pages 18-19)

_____ Monitors children's general comfort and health (see pages 402-404)

_____   _____
Teacher Completing Training Module   Date
(Please sign and date)

_____   _____
Trainer or Mentor Completing Skills Checklist   Date
(Please sign and date)

Congratulations! You have completed Module 8 in the **_Teacher's Guide_**.

Using Anecdotal Observations

MODULE 9

Purpose: to complete anecdotal observations

TIME: APPROXIMATELY 1 HOUR

Read "Observation and Authentic Assessment Allow Teachers to See Children as Unique" on pages 52-55 in *Innovations: The Comprehensive Preschool Curriculum*.

Anecdotal observations of children at play are the foundation of understanding each child's individual developmental pace, unique temperamental traits, and stage of development. Anecdotal observations also serve as a way to uncover play themes and children's emerging interests. You can learn a lot from observing. For example, you might learn when children lose interest in toys and materials or when children need a little less challenge from the environment, toys and materials, and experiences. Additionally, anecdotal observations serve as a record of what is occurring in the classroom (documentation). Finally, observations form the foundation of information to be exchanged with parents during conferences.

Observation is an active process. Good teachers are always observing and then recording their observations to use later as springboards for reflection. *Innovations: The Comprehensive Preschool Curriculum* suggests that you observe children regularly and record your observations using anecdotal records.

An anecdotal record is a specific type of written observation. When making an anecdotal record, include only objective information in your observation notes. Focus on what you see, when you see it, how it happens, where the child is, and what is happening. All of these topics are objective. Do not record what you *think* about what you see; just record what is happening.

The following is an example of an anecdotal observation.

Anecdotal Record

Child Ashley Hill   **Date** July 23   **Time** 9:40

What I observed Ashley walked into dramatic play with her hands on her hips. She said, "I'm the teacher, so you have to do what I say." Ashley picked up the book, The Three Bears, and sat down at the table. Joe and Le sat down at the table, too. Ashley said, "Now don't interrupt me. It is now time for a story. Once upon a time there were three bears...."

Teacher Miss Tasha

Complete the Anecdotal Record below by observing one of the children in your classroom.

Anecdotal Record

Child   **Date**   **Time**

What I observed

Teacher

Subjective Words—These are words that describe the way a person feels about something. Usually there are no visual clues in a subjective description of something or a child's behavior. If it's subjective, it's not really observable and is very difficult, if not impossible, to measure.

Objective Words—The dictionary gives this definition of the word *object*: A thing that can be seen or touched and something that is observable. When making a list of words and phrases that express objective behaviors, we must remember that they are real and factual, not expressions of feelings or thoughts, but things you can see and observe.

Use the lists of Subjective and Objective Words below to determine if your Anecdotal Record is objective. Make any changes necessary to eliminate subjective comments.

Subjective Words	Objective Words
sulking	alone
silly	rolling on the floor while singing
rude	yelled at _____
enthusiastic	clapping her hands
tired	laid on the rug for two hours
playful	bouncing the ball
stubborn	keeps throwing the blocks
afraid	hiding behind the door
whining	cries while talking
rigid	always wants to play with blocks
happy	smiling
helpful	picks up the toys
making progress	knows three new songs
sad	frowning
thought	said
sweet	helped Rhonda make bubbles
friendly	hugs the children when they arrive
mean	hit Harrison with a block
nice	gave Tomeka a hug
patient	waited for the other children
hated	screamed
bullied	pushed
wished	was quiet

Skills Checklist

If you are currently working in the classroom, ask your mentor to support your development by observing your growing skills. For now, ask your mentor to observe only for the skills listed below. Then, as you complete additional modules and learn new skills and abilities, use the complete list on pages 105-107 of this book to confirm that you are developing your teaching skills repertoire. If you are unfamiliar with an item, read about it in the book or talk further with your mentor or trainer. If you are not currently teaching, become familiar with the concepts and save the lists to use when you are teaching in a preschool program.

_____ Is an alert observer of each child in the classroom (see pages 46-47)
_____ Develops and maintains a system for recording regular anecdotal notes (see page 47)
_____ Uses observations to inform teaching (see pages 52-53)

_____   _____
Teacher Completing Training Module   Date
(Please sign and date)

_____   _____
Trainer or Mentor Completing Skills Checklist   Date
(Please sign and date)

Congratulations! You have completed Module 9 in the **Teacher's Guide**.

Innovations in Family Partnerships

MODULE
10

Purpose: to create partnerships between teachers, early childhood education programs, parents, and families

TIME: APPROXIMATELY 1 HOUR

Parents, more than anyone else, influence the children in your care. No matter how long children are in early childhood education programs during the day, their parents are still their primary educators and their child's first and most important teachers. By keeping families informed, listening to their concerns, and welcoming them to participate in their child's experiences at school, you are able to form partnerships with them to strengthen families and support children's learning.

Innovations: The Comprehensive Preschool Curriculum provides many different ways to develop partnerships with families and encourage them to participate in their child's life at school. Read about Innovations in Family Partnerships in Chapter 1—Getting Started, page 19. Chapters 2–7 each include a section called Innovations in Family Partnerships that offers suggestions for family involvement (such as collecting materials to be made into toys for the classroom or invitations for families to come to a parent meeting) and parent postcards (to assist families in understanding and supporting their child's growth and development), and additional resources for families (pages 57-61, 144-148, 224-227, 315-321, 408-411, 498-502). In addition to these suggestions, *Innovations: The Comprehensive Preschool Curriculum* offers additional postcards and more ideas on how to involve parents in every Possibilities Plan. See the Schedule for Postcards on page 112 of this book for ideas on when to send out information to parents.

Family involvement helps everyone. Parents usually have a higher rate of satisfaction with their child's teacher and their child's school when they are involved in their child's education. Children benefit when the teacher and the family form a partnership. And the teacher benefits from the insight and understanding shared by the family, creating the best possible situation to support the child in the classroom. Use the Parent Visit Log on page 114 of this book to track parents' activities in the classroom.

Choose an activity in Chapter 2 to encourage parents to be involved. Write the activity you chose below. Include the page number.

10

Implement the activity. Then, explain how it worked.

How will you modify the activity if you use it again?

Reflecting on the success of the family participation activities that you select will help you modify future plans.

Skills Checklist

If you are currently working in the classroom, ask your mentor to support your development by observing your growing skills. For now, ask your mentor to observe only for the skills listed below. Then, as you complete additional modules and learn new skills and abilities, use the complete list on pages 105-107 of this book to confirm that you are developing your teaching skills repertoire. If you are unfamiliar with an item, read about it in the book or talk further with your mentor or trainer. If you are not currently teaching, become familiar with the concepts and save the lists to use when you are teaching in a preschool program.

_____ Maintains a positive, pleasant attitude toward family members; thinks in terms of creating a partnership to support the child (see pages 57-58)

_____ Shows support for parents as primary educators by developing a partnership of respect, information exchange, and collaboration (see pages 57-58)

_____ Finds many different ways for family members to be involved in the school experience of the child

_____   _____

Teacher Completing Training Module   Date
(Please sign and date)

_____   _____

Trainer or Mentor Completing Skills Checklist   Date
(Please sign and date)

Congratulations! You have completed Module 10 in the **Teacher's Guide**.

Innovations in Environments

Purpose: to evaluate important elements of the classroom that create a positive learning environment

TIME: APPROXIMATELY 1 ½ HOURS

Every classroom has an "extra" teacher—the environment. Because children learn through the active exploration of their surroundings, you must plan an appropriate learning environment for the children in your classroom. Children "live" in their school settings (Greenman, 1996). Because of this, stimulation activities must be balanced across the important dimensions of activity (quiet or active), location (indoor or outdoor), and initiator (child-initiated or adult-initiated) (Bredekamp, 1997; National Academy of Early Childhood Programs, 1991). Integrate information from the Innovations in Environments sections of the book into your Possibilities Plans to improve your classroom environment.

First, read about Innovations in Environments in Chapter 1—Getting Started, page 20. Next, read about Innovations in Environments in Chapter 2 (pages 61-63).

Teachers have the following responsibilities for the environment:

- *Creating the Environment*—Teachers use their knowledge of what a classroom needs to determine room arrangement and the organization of materials.
- *Maintaining the Environment*—Teachers keep the environment safe by inspecting toys and the classroom for problems. Teachers fix or discard broken toys or toys with missing pieces. Teachers keep the classroom clean and organized.
- *Refreshing the Environment*—Teachers plan for different experiences by adding a variety of different materials and taking away some of the old materials. A balance between novel toys, materials, and experiences and familiar toys, materials, and experiences is achieved.

List one way you can create the environment in your classroom.

List one way you can maintain the environment in your classroom.

II

List one way you can refresh the environment in your classroom.

Use the following checklist to evaluate your classroom. Indicate if you agree, somewhat agree, or disagree.

Classroom Evaluation Checklist

	Agree	Somewhat Agree	Disagree
1. Elements are in place that create a sense of calm in the classroom.	☐	☐	☐
2. Sufficient soft elements and nooks help make the environment more home-like.	☐	☐	☐
3. Appropriate places are provided for children's things in the classroom.	☐	☐	☐
4. The classroom is a predictable environment that includes both novel and interesting features.	☐	☐	☐
5. The classroom includes places to be alone that do not sacrifice visual supervision.	☐	☐	☐
6. The classroom includes opportunities for different perspectives (platform, windows, doors).	☐	☐	☐
7. The classroom includes well-defined interest areas (language/literacy, math/manipulatives, art, dramatic, etc.), as well as a place for group time.	☐	☐	☐
8. Materials and toys are stored on low shelves in clear labeled containers.	☐	☐	☐
9. The classroom is a print-rich environment with items labeled, children's names evident, and different types of books available.	☐	☐	☐
10. Stimulation in the classroom can be decreased and increased (light, music, nature sounds).	☐	☐	☐

Next, use your results to determine a goal for improving or modifying your classroom. Write it below (for example, create places for each child to put his or her belongings, or add some soft elements such as pillows or carpets to the environment).

Skills Checklist

If you are currently working in the classroom, ask your mentor to support your development by observing your growing skills. For now, ask your mentor to observe only for the skills listed below. Then, as you complete additional modules and learn new skills and abilities, use the complete list on pages 105-107 of this book to confirm that you are developing your teaching skills repertoire. If you are unfamiliar with an item, read about it in the book or talk further with your mentor or trainer. If you are not currently teaching, become familiar with the concepts and save the lists to use when you are teaching in a preschool program.

_____ Creates stages for play by equipping activity areas with appropriate props and play supports (see pages 149-153)

_____ Provides props, play cues, and materials that children can incorporate into their play (see pages 229-230)

_____ Uses vocabulary, materials, activities, and experiences that are suitable for preschool children (see pages 229-230)

_____   _____
Teacher Completing Training Module   Date
(Please sign and date)

_____   _____
Trainer or Mentor Completing Skills Checklist   Date
(Please sign and date)

Congratulations! You have completed Module 11 in the _Teacher's Guide_.

Possibilities Areas

Purpose: to assess the status of possibilities areas in the classroom

TIME: APPROXIMATELY 1 ½ HOURS

A well-planned and arranged preschool environment has many different elements. The first is a variety of well-equipped activity areas. To identify whether your classroom is well planned and equipped, copy the activity and experience icons on page 40 and cut them out. (Enlarge the icons, if necessary.) Tape them to the places in the room where you find toys and materials of that type. For example, tape the Dramatic Possibilities icon to the place in the room where you keep dolls and dishes.

1. Dramatic Possibilities
2. Art Possibilities
3. Blocks/Construction Possibilities
4. Science/Discovery Possibilities
5. Sensory Possibilities
6. Literacy/Writing Possibilities
7. Math/Manipulatives Possibilities
8. Rhymes, Fingerplays, Songs, and Music Possibilities
9. Group Time Possibilities
10. Movement/Outdoors Possibilities

After you tape the icon signs around the room, see if you used all of the icons. For example, if you do not have a CD player/CDs and musical instruments, you probably did not use the Rhymes, Fingerplays, Songs, and Music icon. List below the icons that you did not use.

Now, decide whether you need additional icons. If so, make another copy, cut out the icons, and again tape them to the places in the room where you find toys and materials of that type. List the icons that you used more than once.

Are any possibilities areas omitted?

Are any possibilities areas divided into different places in the classroom?

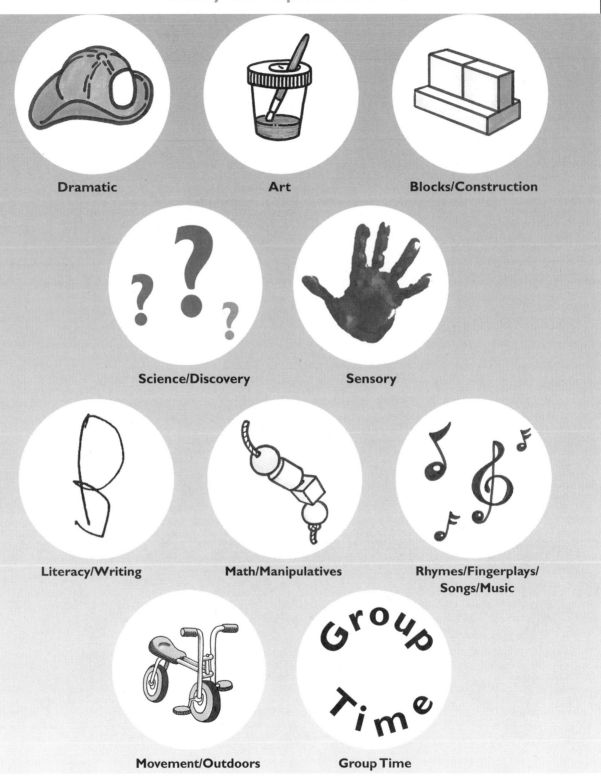

Dramatic

Art

Blocks/Construction

Science/Discovery

Sensory

Literacy/Writing

Math/Manipulatives

Rhymes/Fingerplays/
Songs/Music

Movement/Outdoors

Group Time

What will you need to consider in the future as you create, maintain, and refresh the environment?

A variety of different types of materials and areas in the classroom will help ensure a variety of different activities and experiences for children.

Skills Checklist

If you are currently working in the classroom, ask your mentor to support your development by observing your growing skills. For now, ask your mentor to observe only for the skills listed below. Then, as you complete additional modules and learn new skills and abilities, use the complete list on pages 105-107 of this book to confirm that you are developing your teaching skills repertoire. If you are unfamiliar with an item, read about it in the book or talk further with your mentor or trainer. If you are not currently teaching, become familiar with the concepts and save the lists to use when you are teaching in a preschool program.

_____ Provides props, play cues, and materials that children can incorporate into their play (see pages 229-230)
_____ Invites children to play with each other; participates in play as a partner (see pages 214-215)
_____ Allows children to direct and manage their own play (see page 215)

_____ _____

Teacher Completing Training Module   Date
(Please sign and date)

_____ _____

Trainer or Mentor Completing Skills Checklist   Date
(Please sign and date)

Congratulations! You have completed Module 12 in the **Teacher's Guide**.

MODULE 13

Webbing

Purpose: to learn about webbing and to practice webbing techniques for curriculum planning

TIME: APPROXIMATELY 1 HOUR

Webbing is a method used to identify the many different possibilities for activities and experiences and to create a picture of the direction in which children's learning might proceed. Through webs, you can provide divergent ideas and identify the wide variety of appropriate knowledge and skills for young children to learn. Each Possibilities Plan starts with a curriculum web. Use these webs as you plan for activities and experiences in your classroom, or make your own webs. Because observation is the beginning of planning, use children's interests and skill levels to begin and/or develop webs.

Look at the webs that begin each Possibilities Plan (pages 67, 97, 157, 183, 237, 261, 331, 355, 421, 447, 509, 535). Glance through the activities following the webs to see how they relate.

Create a web of your own for one of the following new topics: Things that Fly, Lights, In the Dark, or Stripes and Dots.

Draw your web here.

When you are creating curriculum plans on your own, you will first begin with observation. Through this observation you can identify particular topics in which children have interest. Then you can begin your web.

Refer back to the anecdotal record you created in Module 9. Can you identify any emergent themes or interests? Write them below.

Skills Checklist

If you are currently working in the classroom, ask your mentor to support your development by observing your growing skills. For now, ask your mentor to observe only for the skills listed below. Then, as you complete additional modules and learn new skills and abilities, use the complete list on pages 105-107 of this book to confirm that you are developing your teaching skills repertoire. If you are unfamiliar with an item, read about it in the book or talk further with your mentor or trainer. If you are not currently teaching, become familiar with the concepts and save the lists to use when you are teaching in a preschool program.

_____ Uses observations to inform teaching (see pages 30, 52-55)
_____ Uses observation to inform curriculum planning and provide insight into interactions with children (see pages 30, 52-55)
_____ Uses webbing to identify the many different possibilities for activities and experiences and to create a picture of the direction in which children's learning might proceed (see page 21)

_____   _____
Teacher Completing Training Module   Date
(Please sign and date)

_____   _____
Trainer or Mentor Completing Skills Checklist   Date
(Please sign and date)

Congratulations! You have completed Module 13 in the **Teacher's Guide**.

Planning Pages

Purpose: to practice using planning pages for Possibilities Plans

TIME: APPROXIMATELY 1 HOUR

Each Possibilities Plan begins with planning pages. These pages list the activity titles and associated page numbers, and other items to support the Possibilities Plan. When you are just trying to find new ideas, you can glance quickly through the planning pages to find the activities.

Use the index or table of contents to find the planning pages for each Possibilities Plan and write the page numbers below as you find them. Then find the related developmental task for each Possibilities Plan.

Possibilities Plan	Page Numbers	Related Developmental Task
Saying Hello		
Castles		
Making Messes and Cleaning Them Up		
Creepy Crawlies and Germs		
Maps		
Spin Me a Tall Tale		
What Will I Be?		
Space		
Foods and Recycling		
Building Up and Tearing Down		
Fantasy Figures and More		
Saying Goodbye		

Turn back to one of the Possibilities Plans. Choose two different activities, turn to the pages listed, and read how to do them. Which activities did you choose?

1.

2.

What appealed to you about these particular activities?

14

Skills Checklist

If you are currently working in the classroom, ask your mentor to support your development by observing your growing skills. For now, ask your mentor to observe only for the skills listed below. Then, as you complete additional modules and learn new skills and abilities, use the complete list on pages 105-107 of this book to confirm that you are developing your teaching skills repertoire. If you are unfamiliar with an item, read about it in the book or talk further with your mentor or trainer. If you are not currently teaching, become familiar with the concepts and save the lists to use when you are teaching in a preschool program.

_____ Assures that all children have frequent opportunities for success (see pages 399-400)

_____ Shows imagination and spontaneity in building on children's interests for developing curriculum (see page 30)

_____ Uses observation to inform curriculum planning and provide insight into interactions with children (see pages 30, 52-55)

_____   _____
Teacher Completing Training Module   Date
(Please sign and date)

_____   _____
Trainer or Mentor Completing Skills Checklist   Date
(Please sign and date)

Congratulations! You have completed Module 14 in the **Teacher's Guide**.

MODULE 15

Possibilities

Purpose: to explore the different types of possibilities in the book and to determine the possibilities and materials needed for your classroom

TIME: APPROXIMATELY 1 HOUR

Read about the different possibilities in Possibilities Plans, Chapter 1—Getting Started (pages 21-26). Possibilities Plans contain the following elements:
1. Getting Ready to Plan (example, pages 65-66)
2. Webs (example, page 67)
3. Planning Pages (example, pages 68-69)
4. Dramatic Possibilities (example, pages 70-71)
5. Art Possibilities (example, pages 72-73)
6. Blocks/Construction Possibilities (example, pages 74-75)
7. Science/Discovery Possibilities (example, pages 75-76)
8. Sensory Possibilities (example, pages 76-78)
9. Literacy/Writing Possibilities (example, pages 78-79)
10. Math/Manipulatives (example, pages 79-81)
11. Rhymes, Fingerplays, Songs, and Music Possibilities (example, pages 81-82)
12. Group Time Possibilities (example, page 82)
13. Movement/Outdoors Possibilities (example, pages 83-84)
14. Projects and Documentation Possibilities (example, pages 84-85)
15. Field Trip Possibilities (example, page 86)
16. Snack Possibilities (example, page 86)
17. Parent Participation Possibilities and Parent Postcards (example, pages 86-89)
18. Curriculum Resources (example, pages 90-93)
    a. Prop Boxes
    b. Books
    c. Observation/Assessment
    d. Picture File/Vocabulary
    e. Concepts Learned

Look back at Module 12. What types of possibilities were missing in your classroom? (Which of the icons were not used?)

Below, write a goal you have for including materials that would allow you to offer these possibilities in your classroom. Create a "wish list" for materials needed for your classroom. Share it with your mentor, director, supervisor, principal, or other person at your school who is responsible for approving and ordering supplies and equipment.

> [blank lines]

Write your goal for adding possibilities here (for example, add sensory, music, and dramatic play toys and materials to the classroom including...).

> [blank lines]

Write your wish list of materials you need for your classroom here.

> [blank lines]

Skills Checklist

If you are currently working in the classroom, ask your mentor to support your development by observing your growing skills. For now, ask your mentor to observe only for the skills listed below. Then, as you complete additional modules and learn new skills and abilities, use the complete list on pages 105-107 of this book to confirm that you are developing your teaching skills repertoire. If you are unfamiliar with an item, read about it in the book or talk further with your mentor or trainer. If you are not currently teaching, become familiar with the concepts and save the lists to use when you are teaching in a preschool program.

_____ Directs children to fill roles that are challenging and rewarding (see pages 396-397)

_____ Assures that all children have frequent opportunities for success (see pages 399-400)

_____ Supports children's exploration by helping them identify the things they need to construct their own knowledge (see pages 401-402)

Teacher Completing Training Module
(Please sign and date)

Date

Trainer or Mentor Completing Skills Checklist
(Please sign and date)

Date

Congratulations! You have completed Module 15 in the **Teacher's Guide**.

Dramatic Possibilities

Purpose: to design, implement, and evaluate the dramatic possibilities area in the classroom

TIME: APPROXIMATELY 1 HOUR

Read about Dramatic Possibilities on page 22 in Chapter 1—Getting Started and in Chapter 4 in Innovations in Environments on pages 227-232. In addition to locating the area in an appropriate place in your classroom and arranging furniture and equipment, providing appropriate and stimulating materials is an important way to support children's learning. Use the list of materials in Chapter 4 in Innovations in Environments on pages 231-232 to inventory the Dramatic Possibilities materials you have in your classroom.

What types of materials do you have a full range and variety of?

What types of materials are missing or need more variety?

Using the results of your inventory, make a "wish list" of items you need for this area. List them in the order of priority. Share your wish list with your mentor, director, supervisor, principal, or other person responsible for approving and ordering materials and equipment.

1. _____
2. _____
3. _____
4. _____
5. _____
6. _____
7. _____

Skills Checklist

If you are currently working in the classroom, ask your mentor to support your development by observing your growing skills. For now, ask your mentor to observe only for the skills listed below. Then, as you complete additional modules and learn new skills and abilities, use the complete list on pages 105-107 of this book to confirm that you are developing your teaching skills repertoire. If you are unfamiliar with an item, read about it in the book or talk further with your mentor or trainer. If you are not currently teaching, become familiar with the concepts and save the lists to use when you are teaching in a preschool program.

_____ Plays social games with children (see pages 215, 218-219)

_____ Structures periods of social time with children; remains available to support, facilitate, or interact while children direct the activity (see pages 218-219)

_____ Directs children to fill roles that are challenging and rewarding (see pages 396-397)

_____   _____
Teacher Completing Training Module   Date
(Please sign and date)

_____   _____
Trainer or Mentor Completing Skills Checklist   Date
(Please sign and date)

Congratulations! You have completed Module 16 in the *Teacher's Guide*.

MODULE 17

Art Possibilities

Purpose: to design, implement, and evaluate the art possibilities area in the classroom

TIME: APPROXIMATELY 1 HOUR

Read about Art Possibilities on page 23 in Chapter 1—Getting Started and on pages 150-151 in Chapter 4 in Innovations in Environments. In addition to locating the area in an appropriate place in your classroom and arranging furniture and equipment, providing appropriate and stimulating materials is an important way to support children's learning. Use the list of materials on page 151 to inventory the Art Possibilities materials you have in your classroom.

What types of materials do you have a full range and variety of?

What types of materials are missing or need more variety?

Using the results of your inventory, make a "wish list" of items you need for this area. List them in the order of priority. Share your wish list with your mentor, director, supervisor, principal, or other person responsible for approving and ordering materials and equipment.

1.
2.
3.
4.
5.
6.
7.

Skills Checklist

If you are currently working in the classroom, ask your mentor to support your development by observing your growing skills. For now, ask your mentor to observe only for the skills listed below. Then, as you complete additional modules and learn new skills and abilities, use the complete list on pages 105-107 of this book to confirm that you are developing your teaching skills repertoire. If you are unfamiliar with an item, read about it in the book or talk further with your mentor or trainer. If you are not currently teaching, become familiar with the concepts and save the lists to use when you are teaching in a preschool program.

_____ Validates children's uniqueness, focusing on positive feelings about their unique qualities (see pages 218-219)

_____ Helps children locate the resources they need to further the discovery process (see pages 401-402)

_____ Provides children with a break from social interaction or over-stimulation as needed (see page 400)

Teacher Completing Training Module
(Please sign and date)

Date

Trainer or Mentor Completing Skills Checklist
(Please sign and date)

Date

Congratulations! You have completed Module 17 in the **Teacher's Guide**.

MODULE 18

Blocks/Construction Possibilities

Purpose: to design, implement, and evaluate a blocks/construction possibilities area in the classroom

TIME: APPROXIMATELY 1 HOUR

Read about Blocks/Construction Possibilities on page 23 in Chapter 1—Getting Started and on pages 413-414 in Chapter 6 in Innovations in Environments. In addition to locating the area in an appropriate place in your classroom and arranging furniture and equipment, providing appropriate and stimulating materials is an important way to support children's learning. Use the list of materials in Chapter 6 in Innovations in Environments (page 413-414) to inventory the Blocks/Construction Possibilities materials you have in your classroom.

What types of materials do you have a full range and variety of?

What types of materials are missing or need more variety?

Using the results of your inventory, make a "wish list" of items you need for this area. List them in the order of priority. Share your wish list with your mentor, director, supervisor, principal, or other person responsible for approving and ordering materials and equipment.

1. _____
2. _____
3. _____
4. _____
5. _____
6. _____
7. _____

Skills Checklist

If you are currently working in the classroom, ask your mentor to support your development by observing your growing skills. For now, ask your mentor to observe only for the skills listed below. Then, as you complete additional modules and learn new skills and abilities, use the complete list on pages 105-107 of this book to confirm that you are developing your teaching skills repertoire. If you are unfamiliar with an item, read about it in the book or talk further with your mentor or trainer. If you are not currently teaching, become familiar with the concepts and save the lists to use when you are teaching in a preschool program.

_____ Is an ally to help identify potential solutions to solving problems (see page 217)

_____ Provides props, play cues, and materials that children can incorporate into their play (see pages 215, 229-230)

_____ Creates opportunities for peer collaboration in activities and experiences (see pages 122-124, 213)

_____   _____
Teacher Completing Training Module   Date
(Please sign and date)

_____   _____
Trainer or Mentor Completing Skills Checklist   Date
(Please sign and date)

Congratulations! You have completed Module 18 in the **Teacher's Guide**.

MODULE 19

Science/Discovery Possibilities

Purpose: to design, implement, and evaluate a science/discovery possibilities area in the classroom

TIME: APPROXIMATELY 1 HOUR

Read about Science/Discovery Possibilities on page 23 in Chapter 1—Getting Started and on pages 415-416 in Chapter 6 in Innovations in Environments. In addition to locating the area in an appropriate place in your classroom and arranging furniture and equipment, providing appropriate and stimulating materials is an important way to support children's learning. Use the list of materials in Chapter 6 in Innovations in Environments (page 416) to inventory the Science Possibilities materials you have in your classroom.

What types of materials do you have a full range and variety of?

What types of materials are missing or need more variety?

Using the results of your inventory, make a "wish list" of items you need for this area. List them in the order of priority. Share your wish list with your mentor, director, supervisor, principal, or other person responsible for approving and ordering materials and equipment.

1.

2.

3.

4.

5.

6.

7.

Skills Checklist

If you are currently working in the classroom, ask your mentor to support your development by observing your growing skills. For now, ask your mentor to observe only for the skills listed below. Then, as you complete additional modules and learn new skills and abilities, use the complete list on pages 105-107 of this book to confirm that you are developing your teaching skills repertoire. If you are unfamiliar with an item, read about it in the book or talk further with your mentor or trainer. If you are not currently teaching, become familiar with the concepts and save the lists to use when you are teaching in a preschool program.

_____ Uses existing materials and equipment effectively (see pages 148-153)

_____ Supports children's explorations and discoveries (see pages 401-402)

_____ Asks good questions that stimulate metacognition or "thinking about one's thoughts" (see pages 308-309, 388-389)

_____   _____

Teacher Completing Training Module   Date
(Please sign and date)

_____   _____

Trainer or Mentor Completing Skills Checklist   Date
(Please sign and date)

Congratulations! You have completed Module 19 in the **Teacher's Guide**.

Sensory Possibilities

MODULE 20

Purpose: to design, implement, and evaluate a sensory possibilities area in the classroom

TIME: APPROXIMATELY 1 HOUR

Read about Sensory Possibilities on page 23 in Chapter 1—Getting Started and on pages 151-153 in Chapter 3 in Innovations in Environments. In addition to locating the area in an appropriate place in your classroom and arranging furniture and equipment, providing appropriate and stimulating materials is an important way to support children's learning. Use the list of materials in Chapter 3 in Innovations in Environments (pages 152-153) to inventory the Sensory Possibilities materials you have in your classroom.

What types of materials do you have a full range and variety of?

What types of materials are missing or need more variety?

Using the results of your inventory, make a "wish list" of items you need for this area. List them in the order of priority. Share your wish list with your mentor, director, supervisor, principal, or other person responsible for approving and ordering materials and equipment.

1.
2.
3.
4.
5.
6.
7.

Skills Checklist

If you are currently working in the classroom, ask your mentor to support your development by observing your growing skills. For now, ask your mentor to observe only for the skills listed below. Then, as you complete additional modules and learn new skills and abilities, use the complete list on pages 105-107 of this book to confirm that you are developing your teaching skills repertoire. If you are unfamiliar with an item, read about it in the book or talk further with your mentor or trainer. If you are not currently teaching, become familiar with the concepts and save the lists to use when you are teaching in a preschool program.

_____ Provides opportunities for exploration, investigation, and development of new ideas (see pages 401-402)
_____ Uses existing materials and equipment effectively (see pages 148-153)
_____ Assures that all children have frequent opportunities for success (see pages 399-400)

_____   _____
Teacher Completing Training Module   Date
(Please sign and date)

_____   _____
Trainer or Mentor Completing Skills Checklist   Date
(Please sign and date)

Congratulations! You have completed Module 20 in the **Teacher's Guide**.

Literacy/Writing Possibilities

Purpose: to design, implement, and evaluate a literacy/writing possibilities area in the classroom

TIME: APPROXIMATELY 1 HOUR

Read about Literacy/Writing Possibilities on page 23 in Chapter 1—Getting Started and on pages 323-325 in Chapter 5 in Innovations in Environments. In addition to locating the area in an appropriate place in your classroom and arranging furniture and equipment, providing appropriate and stimulating materials is an important way to support children's learning. Use the list of materials in Chapter 5 in Innovations in Environments (pages 324-325) to inventory the Literacy/Writing Possibilities materials you have in your classroom.

What types of materials do you have a full range and variety of?

What types of materials are missing or need more variety?

Using the results of your inventory, make a "wish list" of items you need for this area. List them in the order of priority. Share your wish list with your mentor, director, supervisor, principal, or other person responsible for approving and ordering materials and equipment.

1.
2.
3.
4.
5.
6.
7.

A valuable addition to each child's portfolio is a list of books the child has read. Teachers read many books to children during the preschool years, and this list can include all of them. Use the list (see page 113 of this book) to reflect a child's favorite books over time, or perhaps construct a list of the books that the child knows well enough to tell or "read" to others.

Skills Checklist

If you are currently working in the classroom, ask your mentor to support your development by observing your growing skills. For now, ask your mentor to observe only for the skills listed below. Then, as you complete additional modules and learn new skills and abilities, use the complete list on pages 105-107 of this book to confirm that you are developing your teaching skills repertoire. If you are unfamiliar with an item, read about it in the book or talk further with your mentor or trainer. If you are not currently teaching, become familiar with the concepts and save the lists to use when you are teaching in a preschool program.

_____ Encourages language by expanding and adding complexity to sentences used by children (see pages 303-305)

_____ Narrates routines throughout the day (see pages 303-304)

_____ Associates letters with the sounds they make (see pages 308)

_____   _____
Teacher Completing Training Module   Date
(Please sign and date)

_____   _____
Trainer or Mentor Completing Skills Checklist   Date
(Please sign and date)

Congratulations! You have completed Module 21 in the ***Teacher's Guide***.

MODULE 22

Math/Manipulatives Possibilities

Purpose: to design, implement, and evaluate a math/manipulatives possibilities area in the classroom

TIME: APPROXIMATELY 1 HOUR

Read about Math/Manipulatives Possibilities on page 24 in Chapter 1—Getting Started and on pages 414-415 in Chapter 6 in Innovations in Environments. In addition to locating the area in an appropriate place in your classroom and arranging furniture and equipment, providing appropriate and stimulating materials is an important way to support children's learning. Use the list of materials in Chapter 6 in Innovations in Environments (page 415) to inventory the Math/Manipulatives Possibilities materials you have in your classroom.

What types of materials do you have a full range and variety of?

What types of materials are missing or need more variety?

Using the results of your inventory, make a "wish list" of items you need for this area. List them in the order of priority. Share your wish list with your mentor, director, supervisor, principal, or other person responsible for approving and ordering materials and equipment.

1.
2.
3.
4.
5.
6.
7.

Skills Checklist

If you are currently working in the classroom, ask your mentor to support your development by observing your growing skills. For now, ask your mentor to observe only for the skills listed below. Then, as you complete additional modules and learn new skills and abilities, use the complete list on pages 105-107 of this book to confirm that you are developing your teaching skills repertoire. If you are unfamiliar with an item, read about it in the book or talk further with your mentor or trainer. If you are not currently teaching, become familiar with the concepts and save the lists to use when you are teaching in a preschool program.

_____ Helps children handle failure by being close and recognizing effort (see pages 488-490)
_____ Creates stages for play by equipping activity areas with appropriate props and play supports (see page 215)
_____ Demonstrates skills to children, teaching them "how to" by showing them (see page 215)

_____   _____
Teacher Completing Training Module   Date
(Please sign and date)

_____   _____
Trainer or Mentor Completing Skills Checklist   Date
(Please sign and date)

Congratulations! You have completed Module 22 in the **Teacher's Guide**.

MODULE 23

Rhymes, Fingerplays, Songs, and Music Possibilities

Purpose: to design, implement, and evaluate a rhymes, fingerplays, songs, and music possibilities area in the classroom

TIME: APPROXIMATELY 1 ½ HOURS

Read about Rhymes, Fingerplays, Songs, and Music Possibilities on page 24 in Chapter 1—Getting Started and on page 326 in Chapter 5 in Curriculum Resources. In addition to locating the area in an appropriate place in your classroom and arranging furniture and equipment, providing appropriate and stimulating materials is an important way to support children's learning. Use the list of materials in Chapter 5 in Curriculum Resources (page 326) to inventory the Rhymes, Fingerplays, Songs, and Music Possibilities materials you have in your classroom.

What types of materials do you have a full range and variety of?

Name three times during the day when you could use rhymes, fingerplays, or songs in your classroom.

1.
2.
3.

Having the words and/or music convenient in the classroom will make it easier for you to use them throughout the day. Either start or add to your fingerplay file. You may want to start with seven different rhymes, fingerplays, or songs in *Innovations: The Comprehensive Preschool Curriculum*. Place copies in an index card file or a resealable bag.

What types of materials are missing or need more variety?

Using the results of your inventory, make a "wish list" of items you need for this area. List them in the order of priority. Share your wish list with your mentor, director, supervisor, principal, or other person responsible for approving and ordering materials or equipment.

1.

2.

3.

4.

5.

6.

7.

Skills Checklist

If you are currently working in the classroom, ask your mentor to support your development by observing your growing skills. For now, ask your mentor to observe only for the skills listed below. Then, as you complete additional modules and learn new skills and abilities, use the complete list on pages 105-107 of this book to confirm that you are developing your teaching skills repertoire. If you are unfamiliar with an item, read about it in the book or talk further with your mentor or trainer. If you are not currently teaching, become familiar with the concepts and save the lists to use when you are teaching in a preschool program.

_____ Uses existing materials and equipment effectively (see pages 148-153)
_____ Demonstrates skills to children, teaching them "how to" by showing them (see page 215)
_____ Has, uses, and adds to a file of rhymes, fingerplays, songs, and music (see page 326)

_____   _____

Teacher Completing Training Module   Date
(Please sign and date)

_____   _____

Trainer or Mentor Completing Skills Checklist   Date
(Please sign and date)

Congratulations! You have completed Module 23 in the **Teacher's Guide**.

MODULE 24

Group Time Possibilities

Purpose: to design, implement, and evaluate a group time possibilities area in the classroom

TIME: APPROXIMATELY 1 HOUR

Read about Group Time Possibilities on page 24 in Chapter 1—Getting Started and on page 325 in Chapter 5 in Innovations in Environments. After you have read about Group Time Possibilities, evaluate how you use group time during the day in your classroom. List three ways you can make group time a more positive classroom experience for preschoolers.

1.

2.

3.

Skills Checklist

If you are currently working in the classroom, ask your mentor to support your development by observing your growing skills. For now, ask your mentor to observe only for the skills listed below. Then, as you complete additional modules and learn new skills and abilities, use the complete list on pages 105-107 of this book to confirm that you are developing your teaching skills repertoire. If you are unfamiliar with an item, read about it in the book or talk further with your mentor or trainer. If you are not currently teaching, become familiar with the concepts and save the lists to use when you are teaching in a preschool program.

_____ Structures group time to maintain children's interest (see page 325)

_____ Supports children's feelings of belonging—all children belong in the classroom (see page 216-217, 227-229)

_____ Summarizes what is happening in the classroom for children; helps children notice what is happening beyond their immediate play sphere (see page 325)

_____   _____

Teacher Completing Training Module   Date
(Please sign and date)

_____   _____

Trainer or Mentor Completing Skills Checklist   Date
(Please sign and date)

Congratulations! You have completed Module 24 in the **Teacher's Guide**.

Movement/Outdoors Possibilities

Purpose: to design, implement, and evaluate a movement/outdoors possibilities area in the classroom

TIME: APPROXIMATELY I HOUR

Read about Movement/Outdoors Possibilities on page 25 in Chapter 1—Getting Started and on pages 502-504 in Chapter 7 in Innovations in Environments. In addition to locating and arranging furniture and equipment, providing appropriate and stimulating materials is an important way to support children's learning. Use the list of materials in Chapter 7 in Innovations in Environments (page 504) to inventory the Movement/Outdoors Possibilities materials you have in your classroom.

What types of materials do you have a full range and variety of?

What types of materials are missing or need more variety?

Using the results of your inventory, make a "wish list" of items you need for this area. List them in the order of priority. Share your wish list with your mentor, director, supervisor, principal, or other person responsible for approving and ordering materials and equipment.

1.
2.
3.
4.
5.
6.
7.

Often, indoor materials and equipment can be taken outside for a new experience for children. (For example, reading a book to children outside or having dramatic play outside can provide a different and unique experience.) Choose something from the classroom to take outside and tell how you will use it.

Skills Checklist

If you are currently working in the classroom, ask your mentor to support your development by observing your growing skills. For now, ask your mentor to observe only for the skills listed below. Then, as you complete additional modules and learn new skills and abilities, use the complete list on pages 105-107 of this book to confirm that you are developing your teaching skills repertoire. If you are unfamiliar with an item, read about it in the book or talk further with your mentor or trainer. If you are not currently teaching, become familiar with the concepts and save the lists to use when you are teaching in a preschool program.

_____ Provides regular and varied outdoor experiences (see pages 502-504)
_____ Provides ample opportunity for and encouragement of large muscle activity (see page 503)
_____ Helps children find ways to take risks without endangering themselves or others (see pages 399-400)

_____   _____
Teacher Completing Training Module   Date
(Please sign and date)

_____   _____
Trainer or Mentor Completing Skills Checklist   Date
(Please sign and date)

Congratulations! You have completed Module 25 in the **Teacher's Guide**.

Projects and Documentation Possibilities

Purpose: to understand projects and documentation possibilities; to implement a project and identify documentation possibilities

TIME: APPROXIMATELY I HOUR '

Read about Projects and Documentation Possibilities on page 25 in Chapter 1—Getting Started and on page 505 in Chapter 7 in Innovations in Environments. Projects are in-depth investigations that children have over time. Projects are important because they provide continuity of experience and opportunities to explore a topic or experience of interest in a comprehensive way.

Each Possibilities Plan includes ideas for projects. Look on the planning pages or in the table of contents to find the Projects and Documentation Possibilities for each Possibilities Plan.

Choose a project from any of the Possibilities Plans in the book.

What project did you choose? Write the title below and include the page number.

Try the project with the children in your classroom. Below, explain what happened.

Describe the content children explored as the project unfolded.

Make a list of documentation ideas that might work with the project you chose.

Skills Checklist

If you are currently working in the classroom, ask your mentor to support your development by observing your growing skills. For now, ask your mentor to observe only for the skills listed below. Then, as you complete additional modules and learn new skills and abilities, use the complete list on pages 105-107 of this book to confirm that you are developing your teaching skills repertoire. If you are unfamiliar with an item, read about it in the book or talk further with your mentor or trainer. If you are not currently teaching, become familiar with the concepts and save the lists to use when you are teaching in a preschool program.

_____ Provides opportunities for exploration, investigation, and development of new ideas (see pages 491, 505)

_____ Collects work samples that show evidence of children's learning and discovery (see pages 55-56, 143, 223, 313, 408, 497)

_____ Organizes collected documentation materials (see pages 55, 141-143)

_____   _____

Teacher Completing Training Module   Date
(Please sign and date)

_____   _____

Trainer or Mentor Completing Skills Checklist   Date
(Please sign and date)

Congratulations! You have completed Module 26 in the **Teacher's Guide**.

Field Trip Possibilities

Purpose: to gain an understanding of field trips and to plan a field trip to support learning in the classroom

TIME: APPROXIMATELY 1 HOUR

Read about Field Trip Possibilities on page 25 in Chapter 1—Getting Started and pages 219-220 in Chapter 4. Also, read the field trip requirements in your local care and early education regulations. What do you need to consider when planning a field trip? Note: If regulations prevent field trips at your school, plan for a classroom visitor instead.

Next, look at one of the Possibilities Plans in *Innovations: The Comprehensive Preschool Curriculum*. Read the field trip possibilities. Choose a field trip to plan. Which field trip did you choose? (include page number)

What safety precautions will you take?

How will you involve parents?

How will the field trip support learning in the classroom?

Skills Checklist

If you are currently working in the classroom, ask your mentor to support your development by observing your growing skills. For now, ask your mentor to observe only for the skills listed below. Then, as you complete additional modules and learn new skills and abilities, use the complete list on pages 105-107 of this book to confirm that you are developing your teaching skills repertoire. If you are unfamiliar with an item, read about it in the book or talk further with your mentor or trainer. If you are not currently teaching, become familiar with the concepts and save the lists to use when you are teaching in a preschool program.

_____ Sees that children are dressed appropriately for existing temperatures throughout the day

_____ Uses vocabulary, materials, activities, and experiences that are suitable for preschool children (see pages 23-24, 229-230)

_____ Plans field trips that support learning in the classroom (see pages 219-220)

_____   _____
Teacher Completing Training Module   Date
(Please sign and date)

_____   _____
Trainer or Mentor Completing Skills Checklist   Date
(Please sign and date)

Congratulations! You have completed Module 27 in the **Teacher's Guide**.

Snack Possibilities

Purpose: to understand what snack possibilities are and to plan a snack to support learning in the classroom

TIME: APPROXIMATELY I HOUR

Read about Snack Possibilities on page 25 in Chapter 1—Getting Started and on page 416 in Chapter 6 in Innovations in Environments. Also, read about snack requirements in your local regulations. What do you need to consider when planning a snack activity?

Now look at one of the Possibilities Plans in **Innovations: The Comprehensive Preschool Curriculum**. Read the snack possibilities. Choose a snack to plan and implement. Which snack did you choose? (include page number)

What will you need to purchase? Prepare?

How can children help prepare or serve this snack?

How will the snack support learning in the classroom?

Skills Checklist

If you are currently working in the classroom, ask your mentor to support your development by observing your growing skills. For now, ask your mentor to observe only for the skills listed below. Then, as you complete additional modules and learn new skills and abilities, use the complete list on pages 105-107 of this book to confirm that you are developing your teaching skills repertoire. If you are unfamiliar with an item, read about it in the book or talk further with your mentor or trainer. If you are not currently teaching, become familiar with the concepts and save the lists to use when you are teaching in a preschool program.

_____ Uses routines of eating, resting, and toileting as opportunities to maximize reciprocal interactions

_____ Makes mealtime and other routine interactions a time for self-help skill practice and social interaction; makes mealtime a pleasant experience

_____ Actively seeks meaningful exchanges with children

_____   _____
Teacher Completing Training Module   Date
(Please sign and date)

_____   _____
Trainer or Mentor Completing Skills Checklist   Date
(Please sign and date)

Congratulations! You have completed Module 28 in the **Teacher's Guide**.

MODULE
29

Family Participation Possibilities

Purpose: to learn about and plan family participation activities that will help support partnerships with families

TIME: APPROXIMATELY 1 HOUR

Families are so important in the lives of children, and teachers are in the wonderful position to support families by creating partnerships. *Innovations: The Comprehensive Preschool Curriculum* has numerous ideas to help teachers create reciprocal relationships with families.

Each chapter contains a section called Innovations in Family Partnerships. This section includes suggestions for family involvement (such as collecting materials to be made into toys for the classroom and invitations for parents to come to a parent meeting), parent postcards (which include topics to assist parents in understanding and supporting their child's growth and development), and additional resources for families. (See pages 19, 57-61, 144-148, 224-227, 315-321, 408-411, 498-502.) Additional ideas and postcards are included in all of the Possibilities Plans. For example, in the Possibilities Plan *Saying Hello*, see the Family Participation Possibilities section on pages 86-89 for ideas and parent postcards. See page 112 of this book for a recommended schedule to send postcards to families.

To support partnerships with families, choose some participation activities. What ideas have you chosen? Write them below.

How will you communicate with parents about these activities?

How will you prepare for the events?

How will you evaluate the success of the activities?

You can also use a Parent Visit Log to keep track of who has been into the classroom. See page 114 of this book for a sample of the form.

Skills Checklist

If you are currently working in the classroom, ask your mentor to support your development by observing your growing skills. For now, ask your mentor to observe only for the skills listed below. Then, as you complete additional modules and learn new skills and abilities, use the complete list on pages 105-107 of this book to confirm that you are developing your teaching skills repertoire. If you are unfamiliar with an item, read about it in the book or talk further with your mentor or trainer. If you are not currently teaching, become familiar with the concepts and save the lists to use when you are teaching in a preschool program.

_____ Plans, implements, and evaluates regular family participation experiences, parent/teacher conferences and parent education experiences (see pages 57-61, 144-148, 224-227, 315-321, 408-411, 498-502)

_____ Finds many different ways for family members to be involved in the school experience of the child (see page 144)

_____ Recognizes, accepts, and celebrates cultural differences (see pages 208, 216, 227-229)

_____   _____
Teacher Completing Training Module   Date
(Please sign and date)

_____   _____
Trainer or Mentor Completing Skills Checklist   Date
(Please sign and date)

Congratulations! You have completed Module 29 in the **Teacher's Guide**.

Curriculum Resources

Purpose: to explore the resources sections of the book to support learning for preschoolers

TIME: APPROXIMATELY 1 HOUR

Read about the Curriculum Resources that support learning for preschoolers on pages 26-27 in Chapter 1—Getting Started. Then look through one of the Curriculum Resources sections found in each Possibilities Plan.

After reading one of the sections, practice filling out a Possibilities Plan. Use the partial section of a blank Possibilities Plan below and write down your choices from the Curriculum Resources section.

7. Books	8. Rhymes/Fingerplays	9. Task Activities & Experiences

10. Music/Songs	11. Prop Boxes	12. Picture File/ Vocabulary

15. Family Participation Activities

13. Snack	AM	PM
M		
T		
W		
Th		
F		
S		

14. Field Trip Plans

16. Parent Postcards

Skills Checklist

If you are currently working in the classroom, ask your mentor to support your development by observing your growing skills. For now, ask your mentor to observe only for the skills listed below. Then, as you complete additional modules and learn new skills and abilities, use the complete list on pages 105-107 of this book to confirm that you are developing your teaching skills repertoire. If you are unfamiliar with an item, read about it in the book or talk further with your mentor or trainer. If you are not currently teaching, become familiar with the concepts and save the lists to use when you are teaching in a preschool program.

_____ Uses books, pictures, and stories to help children identify with events that occur in the world of the family and the school
_____ Finds new materials to stimulate and challenge children
_____ Uses vocabulary, materials, activities, and experiences that are suitable for preschool children (see pages 303-309)

_____   _____
Teacher Completing Training Module   Date
(Please sign and date)

_____   _____
Trainer or Mentor Completing Skills Checklist   Date
(Please sign and date)

Congratulations! You have completed Module 30 in the **Teacher's Guide**.

Prop Boxes

Purpose: to learn about prop boxes and to make one to use with preschoolers in the classroom

TIME: APPROXIMATELY 1 HOUR

Prop boxes are a way to organize materials that support dramatic play in the classroom. Read about Prop Boxes on page 26 in Chapter 1—Getting Started and on page 232 in Chapter 4 in Curriculum Resources. Many teachers use copy paper boxes or clear plastic tubs with tops. Label the box (for example, pizza shop, airport, community helpers, or zoo) and plan a place to store prop boxes while they are not in use.

Prop Boxes are listed in each Possibilities Plan. Look through the book and find a prop box that you would like to create. Which prop box did you choose? (include page number)

What title did you write on the label of the prop box you made?

What developmental task does this prop box relate to?

What materials did you include in the prop box? List the materials on a sheet of paper and tape or glue it to the inside of the top. Ask your mentor to check the items for safety.

_____   _____

Checked Prop Box Items for Safety (signature)   *Date*

How do you plan to use the prop box in the classroom?

Where will you store the prop box when not in use?

Skills Checklist

If you are currently working in the classroom, ask your mentor to support your development by observing your growing skills. For now, ask your mentor to observe only for the skills listed below. Then, as you complete additional modules and learn new skills and abilities, use the complete list on pages 105-107 of this book to confirm that you are developing your teaching skills repertoire. If you are unfamiliar with an item, read about it in the book or talk further with your mentor or trainer.

If you are not currently teaching, become familiar with the concepts and save the lists to use when you are teaching in a preschool program.

_____ Finds new materials to stimulate and challenge children

_____ Rotates and adapts materials to ensure children's interest (see page 215)

_____ Creates opportunities for peer collaboration in activities and experiences

_____   Date
Teacher Completing Training Module
(Please sign and date)

_____   Date
Trainer or Mentor Completing Skills Checklist
(Please sign and date)

Congratulations! You have completed Module 31 in the **Teacher's Guide**.

Books

Purpose: to explore the importance of books, the Books Read List, and reading to children every day

TIME: APPROXIMATELY 1 HOUR

Reading is an important part of the early childhood classroom. When children have many opportunities to look at appropriate and interesting books and have them read to them by their family members and teachers, they are successful in acquiring the literacy skills to prepare for formal reading instruction in the elementary years.

Read Literacy Learning and Development—Teaching Children to Read and Write (Chapter 5, pages 292-293) to help you understand how children learn to read and write. Then, locate where the books and other literacy resources in your school are kept.

Write the location here.

Now, read through a few of the books to find one you think children would enjoy looking at and having read to them. Write the name of the book and why you chose it.

Keeping a Books Read List (see page 113 of this book) is a good way to chronicle the growing number of books you read to the children in your classroom. Start a Books Read List, adding those books you read to children and the dates that you read them. Then post the list in your classroom for family members to see the reading that you do during the school day grow and grow.

What are the benefits of using techniques such as these to document what happens during the school day?

Set a goal of the number of books you feel you should read to children during the next few weeks. Write that goal here. Ask your mentor to check with you about that time to see if you accomplished your goal. Summarize your discussion here.

Skills Checklist

If you are currently working in the classroom, ask your mentor to support your development by observing your growing skills. For now, ask your mentor to observe only for the skills listed below. Then, as you complete additional modules and learn new skills and abilities, use the complete list on pages 105-107 of this book to confirm that you are developing your teaching skills repertoire. If you are unfamiliar with an item, read about it in the book or talk further with your mentor or trainer. If you are not currently teaching, become familiar with the concepts and save the lists to use when you are teaching in a preschool program.

_____ Uses books, pictures, and stories to help children identify with events that occur in the world, the family, and the school (see pages 322-323)
_____ Associates letters with the sounds they make (see page 293)
_____ Uses vocabulary, materials, activities, and experiences that are suitable for preschool children (see pages 322-323)

_____   _____
Teacher Completing Training Module   Date
(Please sign and date)

_____   _____
Trainer or Mentor Completing Skills Checklist   Date
(Please sign and date)

Congratulations! You have completed Module 32 in the *Teacher's Guide*.

MODULE 33

Observation/Assessment Possibilities

Purpose: to understand how to use Observation/Assessment Possibilities lists

TIME: APPROXIMATELY 1 HOUR

Read about Observation/Assessment Possibilities on pages 18-19 and 30 in Chapter 1—Getting Started. *Innovations* advocates authentic assessment—assessment that takes place while observing the natural course of planned and spontaneous classroom activities. Each Possibilities Plan in *Innovations: The Comprehensive Preschool Curriculum* has a section called Curriculum Resources. One of the resources included in each of these sections is a list of Observation/Assessment Possibilities.

The Observation Classroom Summary allows teachers to summarize their observations for all of the children in the group, pinpointing who needs additional observations and which skills and abilities were observed as children participate in activity areas. Use this form (see page 122 of this book) to note your real-time observations of children at work or play or to analyze your anecdotal notes for the specific observation outcomes included in the various activities and experiences you plan and implement.

When focusing on an individual child, it is best to use an anecdotal record. Complete a 10–15 minute anecdotal observation. Record your observation on an Anecdotal Record. (Make a photocopy of the Blank Anecdotal Record on page 120 of this book.)

Anecdotal Record

Child _____   Date _____

Time _____

What I observed

_____

_____

_____

_____

_____

_____

_____

_____

Teacher _____

Now, look at one or more of Observation/Assessment Possibilities lists in the Curriculum Resources sections (for example, in *Where Does It Come From and Where Does It Go?* on page 443 or in *Building Up and Tearing Down* on page 466).

What skills (from the lists you read) did you see demonstrated during your observation? List them here.

What did you find out about the child/children you observed?

What information did you gather in your observation that would be helpful to share with families?

Did you observe any play themes or interests that might be incorporated into your planning?

Did you get any ideas about how to initiate or modify interactions with the child/children you observed?

Skills Checklist

If you are currently working in the classroom, ask your mentor to support your development by observing your growing skills. For now, ask your mentor to observe only for the skills listed below. Then, as you complete additional modules and learn new skills and abilities, use the complete list on pages 105-107 of this book to confirm that you are developing your teaching skills repertoire. If you are unfamiliar with an item, read about it in the book or talk further with your mentor or trainer. If you are not currently teaching, become familiar with the concepts and save the lists to use when you are teaching in a preschool program.

_____ Uses observations to inform teaching (see pages 52-53)
_____ Structures time for observation into daily or weekly teaching routines
_____ Uses observation to inform curriculum planning and provide insight into interactions with children (see pages 52-53)

———————————————————   ——————————
Teacher Completing Training Module   Date
(Please sign and date)

———————————————————   ——————————
Trainer or Mentor Completing Skills Checklist   Date
(Please sign and date)

Congratulations! You have completed Module 33 in the **Teacher's Guide**.

Picture File/Vocabulary

Purpose: to learn about picture files and vocabulary lists and to begin using both in the classroom

TIME: APPROXIMATELY 1 HOUR

Read the information about picture files/vocabulary on page 27 in Chapter 1—Getting Started and on page 232-233 in Chapter 4 in Curriculum Resources. Also, read some of the lists of picture files/vocabulary in various Possibilities Plans.

Preschoolers are building cognitive images of the things they are experiencing. Pictures help give children a variety of different images and add information to the images that the children have already formed.

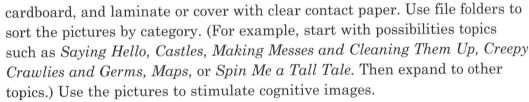

Begin a picture file by cutting out pictures from magazines, calendars, and posters. Look for pictures that show one large image clearly. Trim the edges, attach each picture to construction paper or cardboard, and laminate or cover with clear contact paper. Use file folders to sort the pictures by category. (For example, start with possibilities topics such as *Saying Hello, Castles, Making Messes and Cleaning Them Up, Creepy Crawlies and Germs, Maps,* or *Spin Me a Tall Tale.* Then expand to other topics.) Use the pictures to stimulate cognitive images.

Because the extent of a child's vocabulary is directly related to later reading success, expanding vocabulary is an important consideration for curriculum planning. Vocabulary lists remind teachers to use particular words as they interact with children in the classroom. Posting vocabulary lists will allow families to support what teachers are doing in the classroom.

What picture file/vocabulary categories have you started? List them below along with the number of pictures collected in each category.

Category _____

Number of Pictures Collected _____

34

Category _____

Number of Pictures Collected _____

What's Inside Vegetables
green peppers - seeds
egg plant - seeds, black
  and white "stuff"
carrot - no seeds
apple - core, seeds,
  the apple
banana - tiny black
  seeds and banana

Skills Checklist

If you are currently working in the classroom, ask your mentor to support your development by observing your growing skills. For now, ask your mentor to observe only for the skills listed below. Then, as you complete additional modules and learn new skills and abilities, use the complete list on pages 105-107 of this book to confirm that you are developing your teaching skills repertoire. If you are unfamiliar with an item, read about it in the book or talk further with your mentor or trainer. If you are not currently teaching, become familiar with the concepts and save the lists to use when you are teaching in a preschool program.

_____ Supports children's developing awareness by talking about families, using photographs, and celebrating accomplishments

_____ Devises new materials to stimulate and challenge children

_____ Uses vocabulary, materials, activities, and experiences that are suitable for preschool children

_____   _____
Teacher Completing Training Module   Date
(Please sign and date)

_____   _____
Trainer or Mentor Completing Skills Checklist   Date
(Please sign and date)

Congratulations! You have completed Module 34 in the ***Teacher's Guide***.

Concepts Learned

Purpose: to explain how to use Concepts Learned in the classroom and how to use these lists as one way to communicate with families about what their children are learning and experiencing in the classroom

TIME: APPROXIMATELY 1 HOUR

It is often difficult for families to view the important interactive experiences that preschoolers have in school as learning activities. ***Innovations: The Comprehensive Preschool Curriculum*** has a strategy for helping you share what children are learning with families. Concepts Learned lists are provided for each Possibilities Plan, and you can use these lists in a variety of ways.

1. The easiest way to use the Concepts Learned lists is to copy the appropriate list from the Possibilities Plan you are using and post it in the classroom. When posted, parents will be able to see the content, process, and pre-academic learning that is planned in your classroom.

2. Make the list come alive for individual children and their families by using it to document an individual child's learning. Put the child's name and date next to the concepts learned by that child. Then include the Concepts Learned list in the child's portfolio. See page 605 for an example.

3. You might choose to edit the list from the book, adding concepts learned from other experiences, or numbering the concepts on a Concepts Learned list and using those numbers when completing individual anecdotal observations.

4. The Concepts Learned Classroom Summary (see page 123 in this book) allows teachers to track children's learning of the content, process, and pre-academic skills included in each Possibilities Plan. Use this handy summary sheet to confirm the skill acquisition that emerges as children complete the carefully planned activities as well as to modify the activities and experiences to alternate developmental pathways.

The Concepts Learned lists are important for parents because the lists let them know what you and their child are doing and what the results are. Sharing what children are learning helps families understand their child's growing skills.

Select a Concepts Learned list from a Possibilities Plan in ***Innovations: The Comprehensive Preschool Curriculum***. Observe a classroom for about 15-20 minutes, using the list to assess what one child or children in a small group are learning.

35

Write the skills that you observed below.

Observation discussed with

_____   _____

(Name)   (Date)

Skills Checklist

If you are currently working in the classroom, ask your mentor to support your development by observing your growing skills. For now, ask your mentor to observe only for the skills listed below. Then, as you complete additional modules and learn new skills and abilities, use the complete list on pages 105-107 of this book to confirm that you are developing your teaching skills repertoire. If you are unfamiliar with an item, read about it in the book or talk further with your mentor or trainer. If you are not currently teaching, become familiar with the concepts and save the lists to use when you are teaching in a preschool program.

_____ Comments to parents about strengths, accomplishments, and positive attributes of their child through conversation, notes, phone calls, and so on

_____ Assures that all children have frequent opportunities for success

_____ Delights in each child's success, expresses kindness and support when children are struggling with developmental challenges

_____   _____

Teacher Completing Training Module   Date
(Please sign and date)

_____   _____

Trainer or Mentor Completing Skills Checklist   Date
(Please sign and date)

Congratulations! You have completed Module 35 in the **Teacher's Guide**.

Toys and Materials

Purpose: to create a system for keeping toys clean and sanitary

TIME: APPROXIMATELY 1 HOUR

Toys and materials are important elements in any preschool classroom. Each Possibilities Plan contains many suggestions for the use of toys and materials. A cumulative list of both gathered and bought materials to support the activities and experiences is in the Getting Ready to Plan section of each Possibilities Plan.

Read about Environmental Sanitation on pages 385-386 in Chapter 6. Create a system for the sanitation of toys and materials in your classroom. Describe your system below.

Skills Checklist

If you are currently working in the classroom, ask your mentor to support your development by observing your growing skills. For now, ask your mentor to observe only for the skills listed below. Then, as you complete additional modules and learn new skills and abilities, use the complete list on pages 105-107 of this book to confirm that you are developing your teaching skills repertoire. If you are unfamiliar with an item, read about it in the book or talk further with your mentor or trainer. If you are not currently teaching, become familiar with the concepts and save the lists to use when you are teaching in a preschool program.

_____ Uses existing materials and equipment effectively
_____ Rotates and adapts materials to ensure children's interest
_____ Sanitizes toys and materials (see pages 385-386)

_____   _____
Teacher Completing Training Module   Date
(Please sign and date)

_____   _____
Trainer or Mentor Completing Skills Checklist   Date
(Please sign and date)

Congratulations! You have completed Module 36 in the ***Teacher's Guide***.

Putting It All Together to Plan for Teaching

Purpose: to complete a Possibilities Plan

TIME: APPROXIMATELY 2 HOURS

Read about the curriculum planning process on pages 27-30 in Chapter 1—Getting Started. After exploring all the individual elements found in *Innovations: The Comprehensive Preschool Curriculum*, you are now prepared to complete an entire Possibilities Plan for your classroom. Curriculum development begins with observation. Look back at some of the observations you have made and determine what topics the children in your classroom might find interesting. Next, choose one of the Possibilities Plans that relates to children's favorite interests. Begin by reading the web. Use the web as it appears in the book, use a variation of it, or create your own web. The web will allow you to be flexible with activities and experiences in the classroom to reflect the children's unique interests and skills.

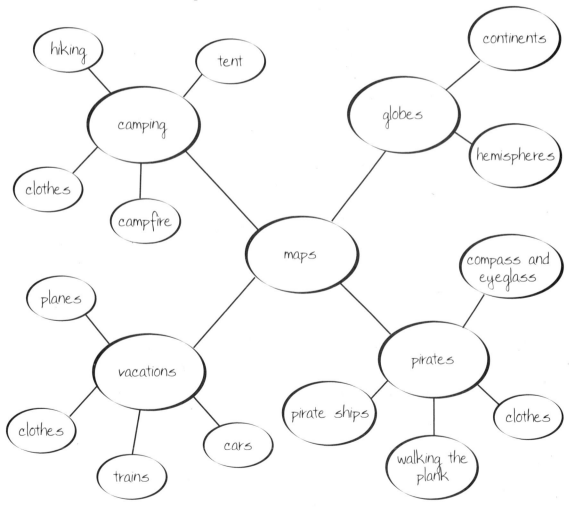

Copy the blank Possibilities Plan on pages 117-119 of this book. Copy your web in the space provided. Use the directions on pages 115-116 of this book to help you fill in all the sections. Post the Possibilities Plan in a convenient place in the classroom, so you can refer to it during the day. Families will enjoy seeing your plan for learning. After you have finished the Possibilities Plan for the children in your classroom, file it to reference as you develop future plans.

Skills Checklist

If you are currently working in the classroom, ask your mentor to support your development by observing your growing skills. For now, ask your mentor to observe only for the skills listed below. Then, as you complete additional modules and learn new skills and abilities, use the complete list on pages 105-107 of this book to confirm that you are developing your teaching skills repertoire. If you are unfamiliar with an item, read about it in the book or talk further with your mentor or trainer. If you are not currently teaching, become familiar with the concepts and save the lists to use when you are teaching in a preschool program.

_____ Assures that children have frequent opportunities for success (see pages 399-400)

_____ Uses vocabulary, materials, activities, and experiences that are suitable for preschool children (see pages 23-24, 229-230, 292-294)

_____ Exhibits flexibility in carrying out activities and experiences (see pages 27-30, 232)

_____   _____

Teacher Completing Training Module   Date
(Please sign and date)

_____   _____

Trainer or Mentor Completing Skills Checklist   Date
(Please sign and date)

Congratulations! You have completed Module 37 in the **Teacher's Guide**.

How to Use Forms to Document Children's Learning, Progress, and Interactions

MODULE 38

Purpose: to practice using forms to document events, progress, and interactions in the classroom

TIME: APPROXIMATELY 1 HOUR

Documentation of events, progress, and interactions in the classroom is an important part of a teacher's job. Through your experiences thus far in the preschool classroom and/or your activities completed as a part of this training, you have already used a number of the forms contained in *Innovations: The Comprehensive Preschool Curriculum*.

Three tools are included in the Appendix to help you collect and use the assessment information embedded in Developmental Tasks and Possibilities Plans. Each is designed to simplify and systematize the assessment process into usable and easily understandable information for families, as well as for documenting children's developmental progress and skill acquisition.

Observation Classroom Summary

The Observation Classroom Summary provides a technique for easily tracking teacher observations. Write children's names on the vertical lines. When you make an observation, check off and date the observation item. You will be able to tell at a glance what observations have been completed for each child. Observations can also be gleaned from reviewing anecdotal notes that are written during Possibilities Plans. When an anecdotal note is the source of the observation data, simply write AN (anecdotal note) and the date the note was written. If you are creating your own Possibilities Plans to supplement the 12 Possibilities Plans included in *Innovations*, identify observation items for the activities you plan and create your own Observation Classroom Summary using the blank form included on page 122 of this book.

Concepts Learned Classroom Summary

Each Possibilities Plan includes a list of concepts that children will learn during each Plan. There are three kinds of concepts: Content Knowledge, Process Knowledge, and Pre-Academic Skills. The summary allows teachers to tell at a glance which children have mastered each concept. Use the blank form on page 123 of this book to identify concepts learned when you develop your own Possibilities Plans.

Child Accomplishment Record

The Child Accomplishment Record is a tool to use when sharing information concerning children's accomplishments with families during conferences or at regular reporting intervals. The Child Accomplishment Record informs parents and family members about their child's accomplishments and experiences at school. It shares the teacher's observations and indicates what concepts have been mastered. It also provides an opportunity for both families and teachers to comment on the child's accomplishments and explore other topics of interest or concern. Use the Child Accomplishment Record (see page 124 of this book) to connect families to their child's classroom experiences.

Look at any of the following blank forms that you have not yet had practice using. Forms can be found in *Innovations: The Comprehensive Preschool Curriculum,* or in the Appendix of this book. If you need assistance, talk further with a fellow teacher, your mentor, trainer, director, or principal.

Skills Checklist

If you are currently working in the classroom, ask your mentor to support your development by observing your growing skills. For now, ask your mentor to observe only for the skills listed below. Then, as you complete additional modules and learn new skills and abilities, use the complete list on pages 105-107 of this book to confirm that you are developing your teaching skills repertoire. If you are unfamiliar with an item, read about it in the book or talk further with your mentor or trainer. If you are not currently teaching, become familiar with the concepts and save the lists to use when you are teaching in a preschool program.

_____ Is an alert observer of each child in the classroom
_____ Develops and maintains a system for recording regular anecdotal notes (see pages 484)
_____ Uses documentation to guide future curriculum development (see pages 52-53)

_____   _____
Teacher Completing Training Module   Date
(Please sign and date)

_____   _____
Trainer or Mentor Completing Skills Checklist   Date
(Please sign and date)

Congratulations! You have completed Module 38 in the *Teacher's Guide*.

How to Use Portfolios to Document Children's Development

Purpose: to use portfolios to accomplish authentic assessment in the preschool classroom

TIME: APPROXIMATELY 1 HOUR

Portfolios show a child's progress over time and can be made in many different ways. Read pages 55-56 in Chapter 2 about how to create children's portfolios.

Forms that you are using in the classroom (anecdotal records, books read lists, concepts learned lists, incident/accident forms, and so on) are an easy way to begin. Gather all the materials you already have, be certain that everything is dated, make copies as needed, and file in individual folders. Show your portfolios to your mentor, director, supervisor, or principal. Ask for suggestions for improvement. Write them here.

Additionally, each chapter has a section in Observation/Assessment that shows items to add to children's portfolios related to the developmental task in that particular chapter (pages 142, 223, 313, 408, 497). Read the suggested additions for portfolios in one or more of the chapters. Choose two things to add to children's portfolios. Write your choices on the next page.

1.

2.

Skills Checklist

If you are currently working in the classroom, ask your mentor to support your development by observing your growing skills. For now, ask your mentor to observe only for the skills listed below. Then, as you complete additional modules and learn new skills and abilities, use the complete list on pages 105-107 of this book to confirm that you are developing your teaching skills repertoire. If you are unfamiliar with an item, read about it in the book or talk further with your mentor or trainer. If you are not currently teaching, become familiar with the concepts and save the lists to use when you are teaching in a preschool program.

_____ Watches and observes children at play and throughout the school day
_____ Uses observation to inform curriculum planning and provide insight into interactions with children (see pages 52-53)
_____ Documents children's progress through the use of individual portfolios (see pages 55-56)

_____   _____

Teacher Completing Training Module   Date
(Please sign and date)

_____   _____

Trainer or Mentor Completing Skills Checklist   Date
(Please sign and date)

Congratulations! You have completed Module 39 in the **Teacher's Guide**.

How to Use Parent Postcards to Support Families

Purpose: to plan for and use Parent Postcards to support families

TIME: APPROXIMATELY I HOUR

Parent Postcards are a way to educate families, validate teachers as educational experts, and keep families involved in the education of their children. Read the explanation of postcards in Chapter 1—Getting Started (pages 19-25) as well as the Schedule for Postcards on page 112 of this book. This section of the curriculum is designed to grow. As you read professional literature, newspapers, or magazines, look for interesting articles that might appeal to parents. Make copies of these to add to the Parent Postcards. When you find an article of interest, identify when it might be useful to parents and send it out at the appropriate time.

You may also choose to write some of your own postcards. For example, you might write a postcard that introduces you to new families, one that describes your philosophy of early education, or even one that tells parents more about the types of experience you have had in early education.

Plan how you will use Parent Postcards for children in your classroom. If you are already in the classroom, list the preschoolers in your classroom and plan which postcards will be given out to the parents of each individual child.

Children's Names	Postcards

40

If you are not yet in the classroom, read the postcards and add one to the collection. Which one did you add? Why?

Skills Checklist

If you are currently working in the classroom, ask your mentor to support your development by observing your growing skills. For now, ask your mentor to observe only for the skills listed below. Then, as you complete additional modules and learn new skills and abilities, use the complete list on pages 105-107 of this book to confirm that you are developing your teaching skills repertoire. If you are unfamiliar with an item, read about it in the book or talk further with your mentor or trainer. If you are not currently teaching, become familiar with the concepts and save the lists to use when you are teaching in a preschool program.

_____ Facilitates exchange of information from families to the teacher and back to families (see pages 57-58)

_____ Shows support for parents as primary educators by developing a partnership of respect, information exchange, and collaboration (see pages 57-58)

_____ Helps parents develop realistic expectations for children's behavior in ways that help avoid disciplinary problems

_____   _____

Teacher Completing Training Module   Date
(Please sign and date)

_____   _____

Trainer or Mentor Completing Skills Checklist   Date
(Please sign and date)

Congratulations! You have completed Module 40 in the **Teacher's Guide**.

Conferencing with Families

MODULE 41

Purpose: to learn about conferencing with parents and to simulate a conference with parents using a variety of materials

TIME: APPROXIMATELY 1 HOUR

Using forms and the children's portfolios, plan a conference and answer the following questions. Then, simulate conducting an actual conference with parents. Ask your coworkers or your mentor or trainer to play the part of a family member or parent.

The Child Accomplishment Record (see page 124 in this book) is designed to gather all of the observation and assessment information in one place to share with families. Complete this Record to support your parent or family conferences and to share with family members the skill growth that is occurring over time. Designed to be used repeatedly, the Child Accomplishment Record becomes the reporting mechanism for sharing what children know, can do, and how they think. This focus on accomplishments and skill acquisition helps families recognize the educational benefits of *Innovations: The Comprehensive Preschool Curriculum*.

Write a sentence to show how you can welcome the parent(s) and put him or her (or them) at ease.

Write three open-ended questions you can ask based on the results of the observation/assessment.

1.

2.

3.

How can you conclude your part of the conference and make the family member feel comfortable asking questions?

41

How will you use Anecdotal Records, Communication Logs, portfolios, and the Books Read List to make the conference informative and helpful?

Skills Checklist

If you are currently working in the classroom, ask your mentor to support your development by observing your growing skills. For now, ask your mentor to observe only for the skills listed below. Then, as you complete additional modules and learn new skills and abilities, use the complete list on pages 105-107 of this book to confirm that you are developing your teaching skills repertoire. If you are unfamiliar with an item, read about it in the book or talk further with your mentor or trainer. If you are not currently teaching, become familiar with the concepts and save the lists to use when you are teaching in a preschool program.

_____ Comments to parents about strengths, accomplishments, and positive attributes of the child through conversation, notes, phone calls, and so on (see pages 57-58)

_____ Spends as much or more time listening to families than providing guidance (see pages 57-58)

_____ Asks questions to clarify parents' points of view or issues of concern before responding with program policies or procedures

_____   _____

Teacher Completing Training Module   Date
(Please sign and date)

_____   _____

Trainer or Mentor Completing Skills Checklist   Date
(Please sign and date)

Congratulations! You have completed Module 41 in the **Teacher's Guide**.

How Can I Continue My Professional Development?

MODULE 42

Purpose: to explore ways to continue professional development and to design a professional development plan

TIME: APPROXIMATELY 1 HOUR

The need to grow and learn is a requirement for all individuals, not just children. As an early childhood professional, you will want to continue your professional development, so you will continue to grow as a teacher and improve your teaching skills.

The teaching competencies, contained under the Innovations in Teaching section in each chapter, are a great place to start. Start by rating yourself on each item as a self-evaluation. You may also want to ask a colleague or peer to use the list to evaluate your performance in the classroom and recommend areas for further development. Also, use the complete Skills Checklist on pages 105-107 of this book as an evaluation of your emerging skills.

Another source of professional development is to read publications of professional associations and to attend conferences. Become active in national organizations as well as in your local community.

One of your professional responsibilities is to document all formal and informal training. Your school may want a record. Additionally, the documentation may be needed to meet licensing or accreditation requirements. Maintain a current list of all training opportunities in which you participate. Keep copies of brochures announcing the training, training attendance certificates, or registration confirmation as a regular part of your training documentation.

It is also helpful to identify how you will apply the knowledge or information you gain through training opportunities. Reflecting on what you learned and how you will apply it deepens the value of almost any training experience and is part of professional reflective practice.

If you have not already done so, make a plan to pursue further formal training and education. Begin work towards your CDA or begin coursework for an undergraduate or graduate degree. Formal professional development is strongly associated with positive outcomes for children in early childhood programs.

42

Write a paragraph below on how you plan to continue your professional development. Provide specific dates, phone numbers, and goals.

Skills Checklist

If you are currently working in the classroom, ask your mentor to support your development by observing your growing skills. For now, ask your mentor to observe only for the skills listed below. Then, as you complete additional modules and learn new skills and abilities, use the complete list on pages 105-107 of this book to confirm that you are developing your teaching skills repertoire. If you are unfamiliar with an item, read about it in the book or talk further with your mentor or trainer. If you are not currently teaching, become familiar with the concepts and save the lists to use when you are teaching in a preschool program.

_____ Continues professional development
_____ Keeps a record of training, coursework, and conferences attended
_____ Participates in professional organizations

_____   _____

Teacher Completing Training Module   Date
(Please sign and date)

_____   _____

Trainer or Mentor Completing Skills Checklist   Date
(Please sign and date)

Congratulations! You have completed Module 42 in the **Teacher's Guide**.

Completion of Training

MODULE 43

Purpose: to conclude training for *Innovations: The Comprehensive Preschool Curriculum*

TIME: APPROXIMATELY 1 HOUR

Today, you begin the final module of your training for *Innovations: The Comprehensive Preschool Curriculum*. Begin by reviewing this booklet for any additional questions you might have. Read the pages that are referenced and/or discuss your questions with your mentor or trainer.

After you have answered any questions, turn to Module 3 on page 12 in this book. Review your personal goals for training. Do you have any goals that still need to be achieved? Use the index to look for additional information on topics you still wish to explore.

Ask your mentor or trainer to fill in your Certificate of Completion on the next page of this book. Post it in your classroom, so parents can see that you have completed your training for *Innovations: The Comprehensive Preschool Curriculum*. Add this training experience to your training records and place a copy of your certificate in your file.

Congratulations! You have completed Module 43 in the *Teacher's Guide*.

COMPLETION OF **46 HOURS** OF TRAINING IN

INNOVATIONS:
The Comprehensive Preschool Curriculum

NAME

SCHOOL

DATE

MENTOR or TRAINER

_____ Participates in professional development experiences

_____ Keeps record of professional development experiences

_____ Sets short-term and long-term goals for professional development

_____ Practices safety precautions in the classroom (for example, attendance taken, children never left alone, allergy list posted, toys and materials regularly checked for safety)

_____ Delights in each child's success and expresses kindness and support when children are struggling with developmental challenges

_____ Recognizes and supports developmental tasks in the classroom

_____ Allows children some flexibility in following routines; does not insist on scheduling compliance that conflicts with individual schedules

_____ Does not treat every child the same—bases interactions and teaching on understanding of each child's developmental age and stage as well as on the child's uniqueness

_____ Uses non-punitive ways of dealing with behavior; can exert authority without requiring submission or undermining the child's sense of self

_____ Waits for responses to questions

_____ Asks open-ended questions that require more than a one-word response

_____ Shows with nonverbal and verbal cues that she or he likes children and teaching

_____ Knows and uses a variety of guidance techniques such as redirection, distraction, ignoring; uses room arrangement and schedules to support appropriate behavior; uses each approach appropriately

_____ Plans, implements, and evaluates parent-teacher conferences, intake interviews, and gradual enrollment

_____ Uses observation to inform curriculum planning and provide insight into interactions with children

_____ Monitors children's general comfort and health

_____ Develops and maintains a system for recording regular anecdotal notes

_____ Uses observations to inform teaching

_____ Maintains a positive, pleasant attitude toward family members; thinks in terms of creating a partnership to support the child

_____ Shows support for parents as primary educators by developing a partnership of respect, information exchange, and collaboration

_____ Finds many different ways for family members to be involved in the school experience of the child

_____ Creates stages for play by equipping activity areas with appropriate props and play supports

_____ Provides props, play cues, and materials that children can incorporate into their play

_____ Uses vocabulary, materials, activities, and experiences that are suitable for preschool children

_____ Invites children to play with each other; participates in play as a partner

_____ Allows children to direct and manage their own play

_____ Uses webbing to identify the many different possibilities for activities and experiences and to create a picture of the direction in which children's learning might proceed

_____ Assures that all children have frequent opportunities for success

_____ Shows imagination and spontaneity in building on children's interest for developing curriculum

_____ Directs children to fill roles that are challenging and rewarding

_____ Supports children's exploration by helping them identify the things they need to construct their own knowledge

_____ Plays social games with children

_____ Structures periods of social time with children; remains available to support, facilitate, or interact while children direct the activity

_____ Validates children's uniqueness, focusing on positive feelings about their unique qualities

_____ Helps children locate the resources they need to further the discovery process

_____ Provides children with a break from social interaction or over-stimulation as needed

_____ Is an ally to help identify potential solutions to problems

_____ Creates opportunities for peer collaboration in activities and experiences

_____ Uses existing materials and equipment effectively

_____ Supports children's explorations and discoveries

_____ Asks good questions that stimulate metacognition or "thinking about one's thoughts"

_____ Provides opportunities for exploration, investigation, and development of new ideas

_____ Encourages language by expanding and adding complexity to sentences used by children

_____ Narrates routines throughout the day

_____ Associates letters with the sounds they make

_____ Helps children handle failure by being close and recognizing effort

_____ Demonstrates skills to children, teaching them "how to" by showing them

_____ Has, uses, and adds to a file of rhymes, fingerplays, songs, and music

_____ Structures group time that is short enough to maintain children's interest

_____ Supports children's feelings of belonging

_____ Summarizes what is happening in the classroom for children; helps children notice what is happening beyond their immediate play sphere

_____ Provides regular and varied outdoor experience

_____ Provides opportunity for and encouragement of large muscle activity

_____ Helps children find ways to take risks without endangering themselves or others

_____ Collects work samples that show evidence of children's learning and discovery

_____ Organizes collected documentation materials

_____ Sees that children are dressed appropriately for existing temperatures throughout the day

_____ Plans field trips that support learning in the classroom

_____ Uses routines of eating, resting, and toileting as opportunities to maximize reciprocal interactions

_____ Makes mealtime and other routine interactions a time for self-help skill practice and social interaction; makes mealtime a pleasant experience

_____ Actively seeks meaningful exchanges with children

_____ Plans, implements, and evaluates regular parent participation experiences and parent education experiences

_____ Recognizes, accepts, and celebrates cultural differences

_____ Uses books, pictures, and stories to help children identify with events that occur in the world, the family, and the school

_____ Devises new materials to stimulate and challenge children

_____ Rotates and adapts materials to ensure children's interest

_____ Structures time for observation into daily or weekly teaching routines

_____ Comments to parents on strengths, accomplishments, and positive attributes of the child through conversation, notes, phone calls, and so on

_____ Supports children's developing awareness by talking about families, using photographs, and celebrating accomplishments

_____ Sanitizes toys and materials

_____ Exhibits flexibility in carrying out activity and experience plans

_____ Is an alert observer of each child in the classroom

_____ Develops and maintains a system for recording regular anecdotal notes

_____ Uses documentation to guide future curriculum development

_____ Watches and observes children at play and throughout the school day

_____ Documents children's progress through the use of individual portfolios

_____ Facilitates exchange of information from families to the teacher and back to families

_____ Helps parents develop realistic expectations for children's behavior in ways that help avoid disciplinary problems

_____ Spends as much or more time listening to families than providing guidance

_____ Asks questions to clarify parents' points of view or issues of concern before responding with program policies or procedures

_____ Keeps a record of training, coursework, and conferences attended

_____ Participates in professional organizations

Anecdotal Observation—an objective written record of the actions of a child or a small group of children over a short period of time (10-15 minutes). Anecdotal observations serve as a way to uncover play themes and children's emerging interests. They also help the teacher to assess children's development.

Assumptions—beliefs or ideas that are taken for granted.

Authentic Assessment—assessment that takes place while observing the natural course of planned and spontaneous classroom activities or by recurring the products and outcomes of children's work and play.

Best Practices—actions or practices by teachers that are commonly held to be sound.

Child Development—a field of study that seeks to understand all aspects of human growth and development from birth through adulthood.

Content Knowledge—facts associated with subject matter explored in the classroom.

Culture—customary beliefs and patterns of or for behavior that are passed on to future generations by the society in which they live and/or by social, religious, or ethnic groups.

Curriculum—defined in *Innovations* as everything that can contribute to the child's development and the teacher's relationship with the child and the family.

Curriculum Planning—the process of observing a child's behavior and then using insight and resources to plan what can contribute to the child's growth and development.

Developmental Domains—interrelated areas of development including physical, emotional, social, and intellectual (which includes language and cognition).

Developmental Task—broad tasks that children must accomplish in order to continue the developmental process.

Developmentally Appropriate Practice (DAP)—using a child's age and stage of development and culture to determine what is appropriate education for him or her.

Emergent Curriculum Theme—a theme used as a part of the curriculum process which have been uncovered or discovered by observing children's interests and play themes.

Guidance—a discipline technique adults use before a problem is present that guides children to maintain self-control without actual intervention.

Interaction—social interchange between individuals, or between objects, the environment, and individuals.

Mentor—an experienced, knowledgeable, and respected fellow educator who can assist in a teacher's development.

Normative Assessment—assessment based on what has been determined through research to be the average or "norm."

Partnership—a relationship where individuals have equal status.

Picture Files—pictures and photographs organized according to subject matter that can be used in the classroom.

Portfolios—method for collecting and organizing work samples and forms to be used for documentation of children's growth and development.

Pre-academic Skills—skills that a child develops in the preschool years that are the basis for later, more formal skills (like matching and grouping skills support later addition skills).

Primary Caregivers—those people who have the major responsibility for the care and education of a child.

Process Knowledge—skills a child develops when learning to do something (for example, pouring water from a pitcher).

Professional Development Goals—specific objectives that a teacher might set to progress in her or his career in care and early education.

Prop Boxes—materials that support a particular play theme and give teachers the play props children need to create a wide variety of roles for children to explore.

Temperament—characteristics of personalities that guide and influence an individual's approach to the world.

Theory—explanatory framework that organizes and gives meaning to ideas and actions, and also guides decisions within a discipline of study.

Webbing—curriculum development tool where the teacher uses children's interests as a focal point to brainstorm the many different paths experiences might take in the classroom.

Appendix Contents

Schedule for Postcards

Begin sending postcards when the child enrolls in school. Select Postcards that are appropriate to the child's situation, the family's interests and parent education and parenting needs, and the school's desire to share information. Postcards should be sent before the need to know and understand emerges chronologically. This makes the Postcards anticipatory preparation for the next stage and, therefore, parent education at its best. Don't hesitate to give parents a Postcard more than once. Repetition assures that parents have more than one opportunity to get, understand, and use the information provided. In addition, some issues arise repeatedly, and it is important for parents to refresh their knowledge of helpful strategies.

Supplement the Postcards with articles, ideas, and resources from other sources. There are many wonderful materials available for parents. When you discover one, add it to the curriculum to strengthen and supplement the topics that are included here.

Parent Postcard Schedule

3 Years

Creating a Separation and Reunion Ritual
We Are Now Partners
Arrivals and Departures *ARE* Routines
Always Say Goodbye
Facilitating Adjustment—How Long Will
It Take?

3 ½ Years

The Importance of Friendship
Making Friends Matters
Handling Pacifiers, Thumb or Finger Sucking,
and Security Items
Being Away from Your Child
What Is Developmentally Appropriate Care
and Early Education for Preschoolers?
Picky Eaters
I Can Make Messes, and I Can Clean Them Up!

4 Years

Expectations with Friends
Setting Appropriate Limits
Participating in Field Trips with Your Child
Managing Normal Aggression in Young Children
Creating Meaningful Play with Recycled
Materials
What Do Children Learn in Dramatic Play?
Managing Change with Preschool Children

4 ½ Years

How Parents Support Exploring Roles
Facilitating a Positive Self-Concept for Your
Child
How to Talk with Children about Their
Artwork
Appropriate Expectations for Academic Skills

5 Years

Good Books for Preschool Children
Using the Food Pyramid with Your Child
Enjoying Meal Time Together
Say "Yes" More Than "No"
Discovering Math and Science at Home

5 ½ Years

Family Television Viewing
I Am Superman!: The Importance of Pretend
Play
Helping Children Differentiate between
Fantasy and Reality

Books Read List

Child's Name _____   **Teacher's Name** _____

Book Titles	Date Read
1.	
2.	
3.	
4.	
5.	
6.	
7.	
8.	
9.	
10.	
11.	
12.	
13.	
14.	
15.	
16.	
17.	
18.	
19.	
20.	
21.	
22.	
23.	
24.	
25.	
26.	
27.	
28.	
29.	
30.	

Parent Visit Log

Child's Name _____   **Teacher's Name** _____

Date	Name of Parent
1.	
2.	
3.	
4.	
5.	
6.	
7.	
8.	
9.	
10.	
11.	
12.	
13.	
14.	
15.	
16.	
17.	
18.	
19.	
20.	
21.	
22.	
23.	
24.	
25.	
26.	
27.	
28.	
29.	
30.	

Possibilities Planning

Although **Innovations: The Comprehensive Preschool Curriculum** is emergent in nature, planning is critical. The purpose of a Possibilities Plan is to focus attention on all of the dimensions of planning curriculum and to support teachers' efforts to make both parents and others aware of the focus, events, activities, experiences, and interactions that are being considered and provided for children. The Possibilities Plan includes all the different components of curriculum addressed in **Innovations: The Comprehensive Preschool Curriculum**.

Unlike traditional lesson plans that provide only activities, the Possibilities Plan provides a big picture of the possibilities that might emerge. It is designed to be a living document. Make additions, changes, or corrections to reflect children's experiences, reactions, preferences, emergent ideas, and changing development. You may find it helpful to write your original Possibilities Plan using one color of ink, and then use a different color to make modifications in the plan. You also can make notes on the Plan to show how the children responded to what actually happened in the classroom.

The following list provides an overview of the sections of the Possibilities Plan. Use the Possibilities Plan as it is (feel free to make additional copies), or modify it to reflect individual differences or preferences in format or space.

1. Web: A sample web is provided for each Possibilities Plan. Use it, modify it, or create your own web including ideas and activities that your children might enjoy, as well as to open up emergent possibilities. Then, use different ink colors to show how the web grows or changes as children show preferences for activities, experiences, materials, and so on.

2. Interactive Experiences: Each chapter in the curriculum includes a list of important interactive experiences for young children. These experiences emerge from warm, caring interactions and are rarely the result of planning or formal activities. Because this component of children's experiences is cumulative, interactions ARE curriculum and as such, belong on your curriculum plan.

3. Observation/Assessment Possibilities: A major focus of this curriculum is observation and assessment. Use indicators from assessment instruments to cue teachers' observation, as well as to create anecdotal records of children's emerging skills, abilities, reactions, responses, and activities. Keep observation tools close at hand to write down notes. Get into the habit of writing the date first, so it won't be omitted.

4. Possibilities: Choose from the many different possibilities provided, remembering the value of repetition for brain development. Space is included for the activities you select; list them on the form here.

5. Environment: A well-planned environment communicates volumes to children and supports children's play and work, teachers' activities and work, and family members' comfort. Here is where you include equipment and materials to make, add, take away, and change to keep the environment fresh and interesting.

6. Projects/Documentation: Some planned activities may have a project focus. List those activities here along with your notes or reminders about items to record or collect for documentation either in portfolios or displays.

7. Books: Include children's books that are favorites and support other literacy activities. You may also want to note books that relate specifically to the Plan's topic.

8. Rhymes/Fingerplays: Include the titles of rhymes that you will be using during the plan and place copies of the rhymes and fingerplays nearby.

9. Task Activities: List the developmental tasks that children are working on in this section, along with any of the specific skills or abilities taken from checklists within the chapters related to the task. Remember that children are working on developmental tasks as well as learning content, process, and pre-academic skills, and this section gives you an opportunity to highlight this interactional work.

10. Music/Songs: Include the titles of music and songs that you will use during the plan.

11. Prop Boxes: List prop boxes or itemize the contents here.

12. Picture File/Vocabulary: Write the new vocabulary words you will be using in this section and indicate the pictures you will add to the classroom from your picture file. Including these items in the plan will not only cue parents that you are supporting vocabulary development, but also that you are adding a wide variety of interest and images to the environment.

13. Snack: Use this space to write snacks that relate to the Plan.

14. Field Trip Plans: List field trip plans here.

15./16. Family Participation/Parent Postcards: Family and parent involvement needs planning as well. Be sensitive to different families' ability to participate in activities by selecting a range of participation activities. Also list the titles of the Parent Postcards that you plan to distribute to parents.

When you are finished considering all of these possibilities, you will have a rich and interesting plan. Then, it will be time to enjoy the educational experiences that you have prepared for the children in your classroom, knowing that everything you do IS curriculum.

Possibilities Plan

Teachers _____   Classroom _____

Possibilities Topic _____

1. Web

2. Interactive Experiences

3. Observation/Assessment Possibilities

2

5. Environment

6. Projects/Documentation

4. Possibilities

Dramatic

Art

Blocks/Construction

Science/Discovery

Sensory

Literacy/Writing

Math/Manipulatives

Rhymes/Fingerplays/Songs/Music

Group Time

Movement/Outdoors

7. Books

8. Rhymes/Fingerplays

9. Task Activities & Experiences

10. Music/Songs

11. Prop Boxes

12. Picture File/Vocabulary

13.

Snack	AM	PM
M		
T		
W		
Th		
F		
S		

14. Field Trip Plans

15. Family Participation Activities

16. Parent Postcards

Anecdotal Record

Child _____ Date _____ Time _____

What I observed _____

_____

_____

_____

_____

_____

_____

_____

_____

Teacher _____

Anecdotal Record

Child _____ Date _____ Time _____

What I observed _____

_____

_____

_____

_____

_____

_____

_____

_____

Teacher _____

Communication Log

Child's Name _____   **Week of** _____

Day	Sign In	Bed Time	Wake up Time	Behavior Change?	Parent Comments	Snacks/Meals	NAP(S)	Activities/Teacher Comments	Sign Out
M						Snack A.M. Y N P.M. Y N Lunch	Y N		
T						Snack A.M. Y N P.M. Y N Lunch	Y N		
W						Snack A.M. Y N P.M. Y N Lunch	Y N		
Th						Snack A.M. Y N P.M. Y N Lunch	Y N		
F						Snack A.M. Y N P.M. Y N Lunch	Y N		

Observation Classroom Summary

Name

Possibilities Plan

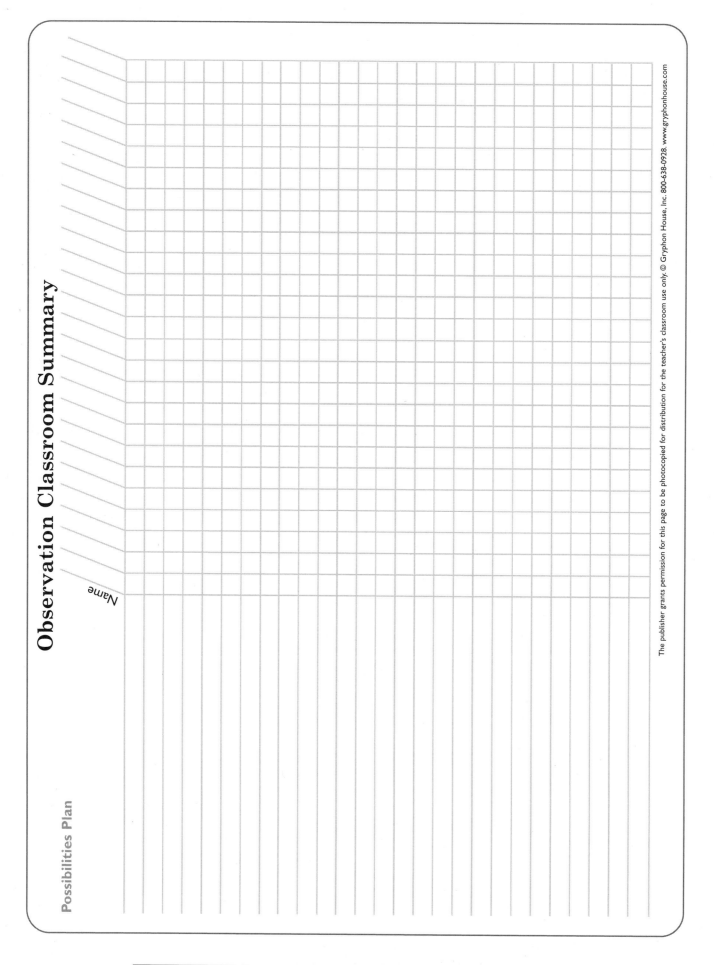

Concepts Learned Classroom Summary

Concepts Learned in

Content Knowledge

Process Knowledge

Pre-academic Skills

Child Accomplishment Record

Concepts Learned for

Content Knowledge

☐
☐
☐
☐
☐
☐
☐
☐
☐
☐
☐

_____

Name

Date

Teacher

Teacher Comments

Process Knowledge

☐
☐
☐
☐
☐
☐
☐
☐
☐
☐
☐
☐
☐
☐
☐
☐
☐

Parent Comments

Pre-academic Skills

☐
☐
☐
☐
☐
☐
☐
☐

Index

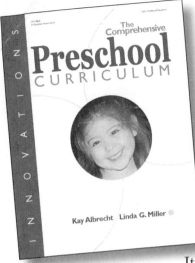

Innovations: The Comprehensive Preschool Curriculum

Kay Albrecht and Linda G. Miller

Designed for teachers of 3- to 5-year-olds, this complete curriculum book focuses on how teachers can encourage, facilitate, and stimulate children's learning and growth. The book identifies, explains, and supports the major developmental tasks of preschool children, including adjusting to school, making friends, exploring roles, communicating, problem-solving, and expressing feelings. It contains a comprehensive appendix, planning tools, and an array of useful assessment tools. 640 pages. 2004.

ISBN 0-87659-269-8 / Gryphon House / 18265

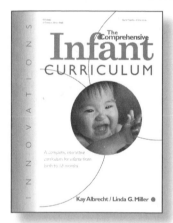

ISBN 0-87659-213-2 / 14962

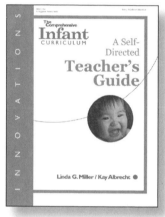

ISBN 0-87659-270-1 / 15384

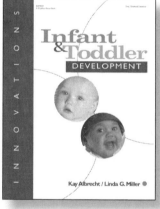

ISBN 0-87659-259-0 / 19237

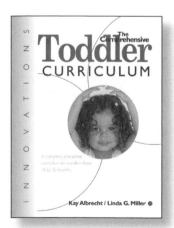

ISBN 0-87659-214-0 / 17846

ISBN 0-87659-233-7 / 16571

ISBN 0-87659-260-4 / 15826

Available at your favorite bookstore, school supply store, or directly from Gryphon House at 800.638.0928 or www.gryphonhouse.com